What Matters Most

Ann,

Enjoy and

good luck writing

Maura Wolf

WHAT
MATTERS

EVERYDAY
LEADERSHIP AT
HOME, AT WORK,
AND IN THE WORLD

MOST

RCWMS | Durham, NC
2014

Design by Designing Solutions LLC
Printed in the United States of America

ISBN 978-0-9960826-0-0

Library of Congress Control Number: 2014942515

First Edition, 2014
10 9 8 7 6 5 4 3 2 1

Copies of the book may be ordered from:
RCWMS
1202 Watts Street
Durham, NC 27701
www.rcwms.org
rcwmsnc@aol.com

For my dad, Richard F. Wolf,
my great uncle, Borden Mace,
and my mentor, Mel King.
They live with great dignity, guided by
their deepest values, and model for me
what is possible in a life well-lived.

Contents

Preface ix

Introduction 1

1 Future Shock 9

2 Let Your Passions Be Seen 13

3 Every Action Counts 15

4 Things That Take a Long Time 19

5 Being Woven In 21

6 Enough 25

7 Deep Listening 29

8 Good Busy 33

9 Leaving Your Comfort Zone 37

10 Get on the Balcony 39

11 The Good Stuff 43

12 Treating People Well 47

13 Transitions 51

14 Working with Conflict 53

15 Right-Size Your Purpose 57

16 What Moves You? 61

17 What's Your Vice? 63

18 Get Out the Watercolors 67

19 Connecting with Nature 71

20 The Nonlinear Path 75

21 The Hard Stuff 79

22 Attend to the Foundation 83

23 The Power of Culture 87

24 Fresh Starts and Strong Finishes 91

25 The Wisdom of Trees 93

26 Let Life Change You 97

27 The Power of Presence 101

28 The Little Things 105

29 Rhythm 109

30 How It Was Supposed to Be 113

31 Drop the Anger 117

32 The Neutral Zone 121

33 Sniggling 125

34 Life in Chapters 129

35 Doing Something Really Well 133

36 Find the Right Incentives 137

37 Get off the Sidelines 141

38 What's the Story? 145

39 Managing Energy 149

40 Flexibility 153

41 The Adaptive Path 157

42 A Wholehearted Life 161

Acknowledgements 165

PREFACE

In his groundbreaking book, *Future Shock*, Alvin Toffler describes the physical and psychological stress that today's complex, rapidly changing world will wreak on human decision making. As our collective human capacity to cope with these forces is dramatically challenged, adaptation is necessary. With the cacophony of information and demands upon us, how do we cope? What needs to change in how we live our day-to-day lives so we can survive and thrive?

As a professor of values and leadership, I have seen the power of giving people tools and language to explore what matters to them most. Bringing our actions in closer alignment with the values we hold most dear is not easy work, as many of our deepest values can remain largely unconscious to us in the face of the distracting stress and pressures of daily life. This timely, long-awaited, and practical book will help you cut through the noise and competing agendas of daily life so you can create and follow your own path. Regardless of your position, role, age, or background, this book is designed to help you bring more of your unique gifts to the world.

Through compelling vignettes, compassionate wisdom, and reflective questions, Maura Wolf offers a hands-on and meditative process for addressing: what ails us, what calls us, what arises as our deepest beliefs, and how we transform ourselves in relation to work, family, and community. The book welcomes and invites us with the opportunity to connect to the deeper content in our lives.

It isn't surprising that this useful and inspiring contribution emanates from Maura, who has spent decades masterfully coaching people to help them uncover their core values, address challenges, and fulfill personal and professional intentions. Recognizing early in her life that leadership was not limited to those in positional authority, Maura understands leadership can arise from anywhere within a system. As a teacher, author, coach, and mother, she instinctively understands the visions that pull us into the future, as well as the limiting beliefs and habits that can hold us back. Maura's combination of energy, experience, and empathy will serve those of us who have grown weary with the effort of transforming our lives or cannot see the pathway to reaching our highest goals.

How might you best engage with this book? Several points come to mind. (1) I would suggest you read it with your heart as well as your head, and it may well be your gut that will affirm the personal truth for you within these pages. Some practices may make more sense to you than others, and stepping outside the bounds of your usual routines may prove valuable. (2) As you begin, keep a journal. The benefits of journaling are numerous, and your life deserves the reflection such a practice will bring to it. (3) Another strong suggestion—share your reflections with another person or within a group. This work of reflecting on our lives is not to be done alone. It doesn't mean that an individual cannot gain great insights for applying themselves to what is most important in their lives, but it can be most useful to have a mirror (friend, coach, mentor, family member) who can help you get the most out of the experience. Identifying who you are now and who you want to be in the future is transformative work, and because we transform most readily in relationship to one another, a real benefit of this book will be to have pairs or groups come together to work through the chapters collectively. This treasure of a book can help you touch that place of possibility within yourself. As working with Maura has taught me, life is too deceivingly short to put off what matters most to you for another single day.

Doug Paxton
Saint Mary's College of California
Leadership Studies Department

INTRODUCTION

I have been musing on what matters most for most of my life. I remember late night conversations when I was a teenager, leaving the glow of a bonfire to walk the beach with my sort-of boyfriend so we could talk about what we thought about the meaning of life. Those talks were followed by midday visits with the chaplain when I was an undergraduate at the University of Richmond, where I grappled with finding my way and wrestled with my concept of God. I struggled to come to terms with why everyone around me seemed to be following some predetermined path, while I felt like I was inside a big maze, bumping into walls and hitting dead-ends. I was filled with passion and desire for meaningful connection and purpose and, at the same time, filled with angst on a daily basis.

I absorbed women's studies classes where classmates and I talked theoretically about how women could have more power, choose good partners, and combat sexism. I was confused that many of the most vocal women in the class struggled to live out their values and ideals on the playing field of life. I, too, felt challenged, which made me even more aware that how we think life should be, and what we are personally capable of, can be worlds apart.

In my twenties this seeking grew all the more heated as I tried to factor in how building a romantic partnership mixed with running a nonprofit that was trying to empower young people in Boston. Exhausted and humbled by failures at age twenty-seven, I packed my bags and set out to interview and learn from other young women around the country. "What choices have you made?" I asked. "What did you learn from making them?" And, "What support helped you to make them?" At the same time as I was doing this external searching, I dove deep internally—meditating, learning yoga, and writing—all in an attempt to wrestle with the questions, "What really matters most to me? And how do I live it out?"

Somewhere near the end of that journey, I grew more at peace with the idea that living into what matters most is a moment-to-moment experience. One that often requires us to come face to face with our insecurities, our lack of abilities, and the demons in our past. I landed on a broad mission to love others. More valuable than that, I realized that consistent daily practice was critical to the process of living into my intentions.

I knew that living my values required effort. For many years, the practices of meditation and yoga supported me to be present to everyday life and helped me to stay on course with the things that mattered. But the birth of my first child somehow complicated the process of discerning what mattered most in any given moment, on any ordinary day. It could have been the sleeplessness or the competing priorities of my work and family-oriented goals. It might have been the many conflicting messages I was getting from society about what should matter most to me as a mom. Or it might have been this new role of being a mom. If being a mom was what I was "called" to do, then I had to work out the details of how to do it in an authentic and manageable way.

Whatever the reasons, the challenge spurred on a new practice. A practice I call chewing on a theme.

Every day that I could I tried to answer the question, "What matters most today?" And then, when an answer emerged, I took it on as a theme to reflect upon, talk about with others, and write about. In addition to helping me get clearer about my values, this practice gave me something to do with my mind as I engaged in the mundane and often boring activities of raising small children. It offered me a way to be curious as I went about my daily life.

I reflected when I was up at 3:00 a.m. nursing an infant and while I was pushing a stroller up the big hill outside our home. I talked to other parents about themes while I was watching a child run endless loops around a play structure at the park. At parties, when I didn't want to talk about the kids anymore, I brought up a theme I was reflecting on to learn how others responded.

I was a mom working part-time, so the things I thought about often spanned both home-life and work-life. I often challenged myself to figure out how a theme was relevant in both of these arenas. I was frustrated that in our society, our home and work lives are so compartmentalized. I knew wisdom from each could contribute to the other.

The last thing that contributed to this practice of chewing on a theme was the reading and writing I did in graduate school. When I gave birth to my son, I was halfway through a Master in Leadership program at Saint Mary's College. In each course, after we submitted standard academic papers and projects, the professors required us to write what they called "reflection papers," one or two pages in which we discussed the integration of our coursework and our lives. I often chose to look at how leadership themes related to life at home. This process gave me a love for the practice and the seeds for this book.

As my children grew and I connected with other parents who craved time to reflect upon their busy lives, I realized that I was not alone. So many of us (parents or not) are consumed by trying to get a meal on the table at the right time, keeping track of the weekly schedule, and getting our work done. Some days, making time for reflection seems totally impossible. I wanted to create this book as a resource for busy people who wanted to take a deeper look at what mattered in their lives and at how they were living day-to-day.

I hope this book will make the reflection process easier by presenting one theme at a time, each with a question or two at the end. As you use the book, I suggest taking two minutes of silence before you read a theme, and two minutes afterward, to notice your responses or questions prompted by the theme. With this approach, a daily reflection practice can happen in just five minutes.

Alternatively, you might chew on a single theme over the course of a day or week and let it sink in. Notice how things in your world connect to the theme. Bring the theme up in conversation and see how others relate to it. Use each theme to initiate conversation in a group that meets regularly.

Here's an example of how reflecting on themes can change your life. For months, my husband and I had been working on our son's volatility. His explosions over not wanting to brush his teeth or go to church or do his homework were sucking the life out of us. In a meeting with a group of moms who were trying to be more mindful, we discussed the power of rituals to help our children and ourselves during stressful times. At the end of the meeting, I committed to experiment with a new weekly grounding ritual for my family.

The following Sunday night I got out a candle and a yoga-inspired CD that I hadn't listened to in years. I turned down the lights and invited my eight-year-old son, four-year-old daughter, and husband to sit in a circle with me. I began by rubbing my hands together and asking them to do the same, slowly pulling their hands apart and noticing the invisible energy between their hands. "Wow," my son commented. I used his response as an opportunity to talk about the invisible impact we have on each other all the time. After that, we spent a few minutes breathing deeply, laughing, chanting, and giving each other backrubs.

I was delighted that they all had gone for it (not a given for any of them). But what pleased me even more was what happened the next week when I suggested it was "grounding time" again. My son hopped into the red high-backed chair I had occupied the week before and began with a poem to get everyone sitting quietly and ready to start. He rubbed his hands together and talked about the invisible energy that is always around us. Then, he proceeded to repeat almost everything I had done the previous week. My husband and I were amazed. My bouncing-off-the-wall son had taken on the role of family spiritual leader.

For months after that initial Sunday night practice, we played around with various activities and took turns leading. Some of our reflection times were led by a favorite stuffed dog and involved lots of laughing. Whatever we did, these times helped all of us settle more deeply into ourselves and into the family. We had begun a new pattern that affected the whole week.

Parker Palmer, in *A Hidden Wholeness: The Journey Toward an Undivided Life*, talks about how shy the soul can be. And how we need to create "circles of trust" in which people sit quietly together and wait until the soul feels safe enough to visit. Sometimes, to determine what matters most, we need a similar kind of patience. The clarity we seek may require a spark from someone or something outside ourselves.

The themes that follow are intended to serve you in just this way. Read them slowly, and see what comes up in response. If possible, share your reflections with someone you trust.

1 Future Shock

I will forever remember the moment when I randomly pulled the book *Future Shock* off a dusty shelf in a library at Mars Hill College in North Carolina. I was in the middle of writing a book, struggling to make sense of how other young women and I made decisions. I was looking for a rationale for why navigating life felt so difficult. Finding this book changed everything.

In the book Alvin Toffler made a convincing argument that the technology age would bring about change so rapidly that the world would experience an epidemic of "future shock." For Toffler, future shock is "the distress, both physical and psychological, that arises from an overload of the human organism's physical adaptive systems and its decision-making process.[1] Future shock would be characterized by a rise in rates of depression, alcoholism, violence, and confusion. Toffler notes:

---

[1] Alvin Toffler, *Future Shock* (New York: Bantam Books, 1971), 326.

> We have not merely extended the scope and
> scale of change, we have radically altered its
> pace. We have in our time released a totally new
> social force—a stream of change so accelerated
> that it influences our sense of time, revolution-
> izes the tempo of our daily life, and affects the
> very way we "feel" the world around us.[2]

Reading those words, I felt that my experience of life
had been named, perhaps for the first time. I experienced my nervous system as chronically overloaded. I
had spent years searching for a way to make sense of
this feeling, and when I read Toffler's book, something
clicked. It wasn't just that things were changing. Yes,
there were many changes—especially for women living with so many new choices. In addition, the rate of
change was altering the way we "feel" life. Many of us
are experiencing life with a nervous system that is in
high gear too often. In this environment, it's no wonder
that decision making feels challenging.

The book normalized my experience. After being grateful to Toffler for framing this experience, I became an
advocate for naming it, and now an advocate for spread-
ing this knowledge and its effects. Now, almost twenty
years since that night in the library, many people take
for granted that we live in this state of increased stress.
But when I first encountered it, it was an uncommon
idea. Since the book was written and widely read during
the 1970s, I wondered why no one prepared me or my

---

[2] Ibid., 17.

peers for how life was going to feel. Why did I have to struggle through so many years of feeling like the odd one out, when many of the people around me were experiencing as much change and stress as I was?

One of the ways future shock affects us is that it obscures what's most important. When I am nervous about job security, anxious about my kids' too-busy schedules, and feeling like I have little support to help me lower my stress level, it's very hard to discern what matters most in any given moment. I'm too busy worrying, distracting myself, or feeling isolated to direct my day and my life from the inside out.

From my work as a coach, a yoga teacher, and a parent, it is clear to me that most people need help working with the stress that goes along with living in this moment in history. It would help if we could all be a bit more transparent about the impact of stress on our lives, build in more resources and support for dealing with it, and see it as a key challenge of our time. My hope for this book is that it will be just that. You may need a small island of time in your day or your week that enables you to pull up from your day-to-day activities in order to see the big picture. From that wider view, you might be able to make more conscious choices about how you spend your time, who you spend it with, and the support you need along the way.

How are you affected by the rate of change? Is anxiety something familiar to you? Does noticing that anxiety in part results from environmental factors help? If so, how?

2 Let Your Passions Be Seen

One day when I was at the zoo with my friend Megan, she called out to her oldest daughter who was imitating the baboons in an attempt to get them talking. When the girl ran to her mom, Megan grabbed her, squeezed her tightly, and whispered in her ear, "I love you." After she released her daughter, she turned to me and said, "Isn't she amazing?"

She wasn't bragging. It was more like she was saying, "I am in awe of this person." I had two reactions. The first was a feeling of inspiration and appreciation. It was really moving to see a mom show her love so fully.

But then I felt jealous. I knew I felt the same way about my kids, but I didn't think I could show it in public. I imagined people would think me as too forward or weird.

Noticing I didn't feel that Megan's gesture was too forward or weird made me wonder if maybe I was just hiding, needlessly keeping my passion under a bucket while I moved through my days.

My kids mean the world to me, and while many people would assume or know it, that isn't the same as me affectionately tackling my son or daughter and showing them.

Every one of us has things and people we care about deeply. For one person I know it's music and hard work. For another it is developing a new anti-cancer drug, Boy Scouts, and making pasta. For a third it's getting through her day sober, so she can provide new opportunities for her kids.

I don't know what these things are for you, but I know they exist. If we sat down to talk for a while, eventually you would talk about something and your energy would shift. At some point we would stumble upon a topic or story that would cause your eyes to brighten. I would know then that I was being shown a door into your passions.

Before this day ends, what is one simple, ordinary action you can take to more boldly show your passions?

3 Every Action Counts

Leadership theorist Meg Wheatley notes that new discoveries in quantum physics are influencing the way we understand change. Though scientists once thought things (like atoms) were separate from and could remain uninfluenced by one another, they now believe they were wrong. Wheatley writes:

> Changes in small places also affect the global system, not through incrementalism, but because every small system participates in an unbroken wholeness.... We never know how our small activities will affect others through the invisible fabric of our connectedness.[1]

She also says:

> I know of no better theory to explain the sudden fall of the Berlin Wall. Before that event,

---

[1] Margaret J. Wheatley, *Leadership and the New Science: Discovering Order in a Chaotic World* (San Francisco: Berrett-Koehler Publishers, Inc., 1999), 45.

there were many small changes going on throughout East Germany, most of which were not visible to anyone beyond their immediate neighborhood. But each small act of defiance or new way of behaving occurred within a whole fabric. Each small act was connected invisibly to all others.[2]

Wheatley's understanding of connectedness gives me a sense of peace. I get such relief from the notion that I don't have to do it all, that my tiny actions connect to lots of other small actions. Without that, so many problems appear insurmountable.

When I was a parent of young children, I had very little time to tackle anything outside my home. All of my energy went to tending to the basic needs of the little people around me. I battled daily with the awareness that the world was teeming with serious social issues that needed attention, but felt powerless to act on them.

Even simple things felt challenging. When my kids were very young, I was even frustrated that I couldn't seem to get it together to compost our kitchen waste. Week after week, I felt guilty about the apple and banana peels that went into the garbage along with the watermelon rind. I was that oblivious environmental enemy who caused the islands of garbage piling up in our oceans.

---

[2] Ibid., 44.

Thinking about my non-action in an isolated way was depressing. But as I began to view my actions within the larger society I was part of, I could see that I was making significant contributions in other ways. In relation to environmental issues, I was making time to listen deeply to my environmentalist friends when they needed someone to help them problem solve. I walked my kids to school and exposed them to nature. I opened my heart to feel my connection to trees. I consulted with environmental organizations and helped them do their work better. Even if I couldn't figure out how to take the steps to start a compost pile, I was taking other steps.

Seeing life as part of an unbroken wholeness reinforces my belief that every action counts. In order to make a difference, you don't have to start a new project or revamp your company. You only need to do what you can. Maybe it's forgiving someone, writing a check, or standing up to a bully. Whatever the action, if driven by your deepest values, it will ripple out in unpredictable and positive ways.

What would happen if you believed that every action matters—no matter how ordinary, invisible, or under-appreciated? What's an action that you feel called to take today?

4 Things That Take a Long Time

When I was in my late twenties, my mother decided that she and I should take a trip to Italy. On our first day we traveled by bus to the center of Florence where the Duomo towers majestically above the city. This awesome architectural structure was designed and built between 1296 and 1436. As we walked around it, my mom began her litany of historical facts. Among them, "Imagine, it took more than 100 years to take this concept and make it a reality."

As I took in that fact, I thought back to my life in Boston and my many projects there. I was connected to a group starting a charter school and another group launching a tutoring program. How would these projects be changed, I wondered, if the people involved were setting their sights on something that might last hundreds of years and take more than their lifetime to build?

It was a revolutionary thought, the idea of working on something that very well might not come to fruition in my lifetime. That, I realized, represented staying power. And it reminded me of a very different process, which required a similar type of patience—making maple syrup.

All through my childhood my dad watched the temperature rise and fall. When the right combination of cold and warm weather occurred, he knew the sap would be running. At that moment he'd hammer a spout into each of our maple trees and hang a big metal pail to collect the sap. By the end of the week each would yield forty gallons of sap. Then he'd sit by a fire that he would tend for more than twenty-four hours straight, stirring and occasionally testing, until the consistency was just right.

Finally, he would arrive back indoors with one gallon of magical sauce for our pancakes and oatmeal. From my six- or seven-year-old perspective, this was something that took almost forever but was totally worth the wait. It was something that lasted, each year taking us all the way through until the sap started running again.

Have you ever worked on something that took a long, long time? Is there something you can imagine working on in that way that might be worth the investment of your time?

5 Being Woven In

I've attended two funerals recently, both for people who were tightly woven into their communities. They were leaders in their church, their work, and their families. Their connectedness inspired me and made me want more of it in my life.

The first was for my sister-in-law's mother, who died suddenly. At the time she died, she was a vibrant participant in her church and her town. She sang in the choir and attended weekly bird-watching walks on land she had donated to the town. She was also heavily engaged in the life of her grandchildren. When I was last at her home, she was hosting a group of people taking a video-based course on Ancient Greece. It was no surprise to me that with little notice dozens of people at the church mobilized to sing, provide food, and speak at her funeral.

In the second case, the man who died was a good friend who lived many miles away. News of his sudden death spread like wildfire through social media. Usually an infrequent user of Facebook, I became an hourly visitor as friends from all over the country chimed in to comment on how John's life had affected them, and how shocked they were by his passing.

At his funeral, one friend told a story of the Sunday brunch ritual they shared. Another friend painted a picture of John as a dad, a devoted husband, and a man who was constantly thinking about community and connection. His boss spoke privately to me about the way he constantly connected people through learning forums and courses.

In both of these instances, the large churches where the memorial services took place were packed.

When I look at my life in comparison, I feel disconnected. I want to be part of a church, but I can find fault with the ten that are close enough for me to consider. I like the idea of joining a community group, but fear it might ask too much of me. These barriers remind me of words my friend Jenny said when I was talking with her about making new friendships on the West Coast. She encouraged me, saying, "Being really close to people isn't always easy or neat, because we are human beings, and human beings are messy, imperfect, and not always easy to be around. But it's always worth it."

Attending these funerals reminded me that whatever the cost of connecting and contributing, when it's all said and done, it may be the most important thing I can do.

In what way are you woven in with people or groups? What gets difficult about being woven in? In what ways does being woven in serve you?

6 **Enough**

As a person who has studied leadership and now teaches it, I've thought a lot about what other people think leadership is, and what I think it is. Many years ago I rejected the idea that leadership was about position and positional authority. It made sense to me that anyone, in any position, could exert influence that would increase the likelihood of change. As a person with a spiritual outlook on life, I also developed the belief that our influence doesn't have to be visible or tangible in order to matter. These ideas led me to define everyday leadership as the process of acting on our deepest concerns and interests in simple, ordinary ways.

As I compare this definition of leadership with what is most often valued, I notice a wide gap. Too often, in our culture, big matters and small doesn't. Extraordinary counts and ordinary doesn't. Visible public actions are acknowledged and celebrated, and private ones aren't. In sports, entertainment, and business, we celebrate the people and organizations that tackle big, extraordinary, visible tasks and leave the majority of everyday actions out of the conversation. It's no surprise, then, that many people feel like who they are and what they do is not "enough."

One year, with the help of a spiritual teacher and a regular meditation practice, I was able to witness myself grappling with the anxiety and tension that resulted from trying to do too much. I slowed down enough to notice that I often worried about work that wasn't done, to do's I hadn't gotten to, and parts of my home that were full of clutter.

That year, I set an intention to make life more manageable. I wanted to do a better job modeling peacefulness and presence. I wanted to do less, to feel less overwhelmed, and to have more spaciousness in my days. I knew that if I wanted the world to be more peaceful, I had to move in that direction myself. I went about this process systematically, trying to cut things out, minimizing my expectations, and saying no to requests whenever possible.

As the weeks went on, I discovered that one belief had been driving all of my activity and overextension: I believed that without all that clutter and busyness I was not enough. I wasn't a good enough mother, so I had to put extra energy into birthday party planning. I wasn't a good enough friend, so I had to call every other week to remind people I loved them. I wasn't good enough at my role in the PTA, so I had to volunteer to hang flyers even though I didn't have time. And I had to put in extra hours at work, so people wouldn't find out I wasn't enough.

Slowly, gently, I reminded myself that I was enough. I just happened to be trapped in a culture that had unrealistic expectations for what we can accomplish. Eventually, I began to let go of this belief and to fully embrace this new idea of enough-ness. As I did this, subtle shifts occurred. When I caught myself starting to race forward, I gently reminded myself that I didn't need to prove anything right now. I could let go of needing to do more and accept that I was enough.

How do you relate to these beliefs: I am not enough or what I am doing is not enough? Do they influence your actions? What might happen if you adopted a new way of viewing yourself and your contributions?

7 Deep Listening

O, The Oprah Magazine, always ends with a one-page article by Oprah on something she knows for sure. What I love abut this column is that it often makes me feel like I'm sitting in a room with her and she's speaking directly to me. It gets me thinking about what I know for sure.

It's not always easy to figure out what I know, to get clear on what I think. At one point in my writing journey I had a visit with Arrington, a close and long-term friend I can talk with about almost anything. At the time I was feeling stuck writing this book. When we were talking, I shared my feelings about writing. I expressed frustration over not having more support at home, urgency to get the book finished after years of work, and excitement over the possibility of making time to write. At the end of my rambling monologue, I knew something for sure. It was time to finish this project! It was time to clear the calendar, prioritize my writing time, ask for more child-care and help at home, and get it done.

To get to this clarity, I needed the support and listening ear of someone who can listen really well. Arrington's compassionate and non-judgmental attitude and her willingness to be present with whatever I had to say gave me permission to babble, to be inconsistent, to be emotional, and eventually to find my own clarity. Once this clarity arrived and I spoke it out loud, I knew exactly what I needed to do.

Being listened to, really listened to, is something most of us need. As a coach and consultant, I have the honor of listening deeply when a client begins to discuss a difficult or emotionally charged topic. I work to maintain a non-judgmental attitude and to be interested in the person's whole story. I've noticed that when people feel deeply listened to, they often feel able to speak their deepest truths, sometimes for the first time.

There are many ways to find a listening ear. Prayer and writing in my journal can help me feel that I've been listened to well. I think of prayer as speaking my truth to God. Writing is a way to work through my truths while witnessing them myself.

A friend of mine used Oprah's practice as inspiration for a discussion among a circle of friends. She asked each person to say one thing they knew for sure. One after another, some of the smartest, most compassionate leaders I know articulated what was true for them in their personal, professional, and political lives. Their honesty charged the room with energy and thoughtfulness. It convinced me that it helps each one of us when we take time to think about what we know for sure and, at some point, to speak up about it.

What is one thing you know for sure? With whom might you share that truth today?

8 Good Busy

My friend Julia Scatliff O'Grady has been fascinated with the idea of time for most of her life. In her book, *Good Busy*, she describes ten people's busy lives and their varied approaches to juggling multiple demands and limited time.

One mother in the book experiences life as though she were driving through "a tunnel." She feels constricted (as parents of young children often do) and realizes that the tunnel won't last forever. A history professor speaks to "geological time," or how we experience time when we remember the millions of years that have come before and will follow our lifetimes. A dairy farmer, a music producer, and a bus driver all experience and relate to time in still other ways.

At the heart of the book lies the question of how we relate to being busy. O'Grady notes, "If being busy is now the predominant paradigm for our relationship with time, then surely there is a way to experience good busyness in our everyday lives."[1]

As I contemplate my relationship to time and busyness, the idea of groundedness seems useful. I can feel good during a busy time when my feet are solidly on the ground, when I feel clear and have a plan for the next few months. In those times I can breathe easy. In that state I can do many things without feeling scattered. I can wrap gifts and listen to a podcast, while occasionally putting down the scissors to write a note about a work proposal, and it all feels fine. When I'm not feeling grounded, I feel tense and agitated and nothing seems to go right. In that state, the only productive thing to do is to notice my off-centeredness and focus on getting grounded again.

Noticing this about my relationship with time has made me reflect on how important "extra room" is for my week. In my world this means preserving white space in my calendar, time that has not been spoken for or assigned a purpose, time that can be used for whatever comes along. For example, I try to preserve Wednesdays as catch-up day. If the house is a mess, I use part of the day to clean up. If I'm behind on a big work project, I carve out a couple of hours to dive in and finish it. If I'm feeling anxious, I might use part of the day for a walk or a talk with a friend.

---

[1] Julia Scatliff O'Grady, *Good Busy: Productivity, Procrastination, and the Endless Pursuit of Balance* (Durham, NC: RCWMS Press, 2012), 4.

Since I never know when something unexpected may pop up and throw my plan off balance, I find it help-ful to scatter little bits of "extra room" throughout the week. I can't plan if or when a kid is going to melt down, or when a work project is going to hit a rocky patch. Without extra room, these challenges can have a terrible effect on how I feel. I need to build in time for "whatever is needed" so that I can be busy, and still feel good.

How do you relate to time? What does good busy look like in your life? Can you get some of it today?

9 Leaving Your Comfort Zone

In my twenties, I jumped head first into experiences that stretched my comfort zone. I did Outward Bound, lived in crime-ridden neighborhoods, and attended intense yoga trainings. I moved into closet-sized rooms so I could afford to write and agreed to all kinds of new experiences with people I barely knew. There was great value in this process. I became more courageous, I met an incredible diversity of people, I learned firsthand about living in a place you don't feel safe, and I moved beyond many limiting beliefs.

After the birth of my first child, things changed. I became more fearful and less willing to leave my comfort zone and try new things.

For example, not long after the delivery of my son, Will, I needed a root canal. Sitting in the chair waiting for the dentist, I admitted to the assistant that I was terrified. I flashed back on the thirty-six hours of labor—the panic

I felt over the pain and my fear that it would never stop. As I sat in the dentist chair, preparing for a procedure that might also be painful, my whole body recoiled. I asked for drugs to help calm me down.

For a while, I witnessed a similar reaction in my body whenever I thought about jumping into a cold pool or going to an intimidating work meeting. It may be that labor and motherhood pushed me so far past my comfort zone that leaving it again felt like more than I could handle.

The good news is that we can recover from challenging and traumatic experiences. Not wanting my world to be permanently diminished, I went to a therapist who helped me learn to go easy on myself. Understanding that being a parent had pushed me significantly out of my comfort zone helped me to relax. I set my intention to be patient with myself. After a while, I became less afraid and more willing to venture further out of my comfort zone again. Now, on most days, I feel back to my old self, ready to take on challenges and stretch myself in new ways.

What do you notice about your relationship to your comfort zone? Do you know when you are in it? Are you willing to stretch out of it?

10 **Get on the Balcony**

Harvard Professor Ron Heifetz and his colleagues have been studying problem solving. They point out that in this new era of complexity and rapid change, it is important to distinguish between technical challenges, those for which we know the solution (fixing a light bulb), and adaptive challenges, or those for which there is no known solution (how to stop oil flowing from the BP oil spill).

Whatever the challenge, Heifetz and his group suggest "getting on the balcony" as a critical step in the process of analyzing a problem and coming up with solutions. This image refers to the process of taking yourself off the dance floor and walking upstairs for a view of the action from above. In *The Practice of Adaptive Leadership*, they highlight one of the challenges in this process:

> Collecting all the data that is out there to see, find, and discover is a critical first step. It is

> not that easy to watch what is going on. It is
> hard to observe objectively while you are in the
> middle of the action in an organization.[1]

I tried this approach when my son and I were having a struggle over how much time he was allowed to watch videos each day. I brought up the subject one day as I walked him to school. We were having a pleasant walk, listening to music he likes, playfully bumping into each other as we walked along. After weeks of trying to figure out why he had so little self-control with video limits, I was feeling somewhat defeated and lost. "What do you think is going on with the video stuff?" I asked calmly and compassionately. "I don't know," he said at first. Then after a long silence, he said quietly, "I hate not fitting in," his voice cracking as he spoke.

I was surprised and silent, as I realized that the critical piece of information in this puzzling situation had just been revealed. I had incorrectly assumed the problem was all about self-control and respect for authority. I hadn't realized that acceptance by his peers was such a big factor in his behavior.

Clearly, I needed a different approach. I recalled other instances in which I had perceived the problem to be his willfulness, when the issue was his sensitivity. From this new perspective, I could see more clearly what steps to take.

---

[1] Ronald A. Heifetz, Andrew Grashow, and Marty Linsky, *The Practice of Adaptive Leadership: Tools and Tactics for Changing Your Organization and the World* (Boston: Harvard Business School Publishing, 2009), 33.

Whether you are trying to assess a conflict at home or trying to understand a complex technical issue at work, it takes discipline and practice to pull away and get onto the balcony for a fuller view.

What is a current issue that could benefit from getting a bigger perspective on it? How might you step back today and see this issue from a different vantage point?

11 The Good Stuff

Looking out my mother-in-law's window one morning, I reflected on how well she cultivates beauty. Her garden blooms with exquisite flowers in the spring and summer. Inside the house she has picked just the right robin's egg blue for a dining room wall. This morning she wrapped a gift with clear cellophane and a simple green bow to make it lovely. Noticing this, amid a very challenging holiday visit, reminded me that my husband got from her a deep love of beauty. Turning my attention to this positive aspect of him and his family began to turn my day around.

Our families can be challenging. We share so much history, and we all develop attachments to how we want other members to be and behave. Sometimes our families provide the perfect comfort or inspiration. At other times they may challenge us more than anyone else. Sometimes it requires strong discipline to turn away from the negativity to notice the best of what they offer, and let the rest go.

While I could list many aspects of my life growing up that were not so desirable, I have spent more than enough time noticing those things. I get more joy from turning my attention to the good stuff. From my dad I got a capacity for hard work. From my mom I got an appreciation for the spiritual dimensions of life. It's no surprise that I'm most contented and productive when I'm working hard on something that has a spiritual aspect to it. These values were planted early and deeply into who I am.

When I think about the family I'm creating with my husband and children, I don't know what my kids might look back on and value. However, I have found it helpful to notice what we are good at now and try to nurture those strengths.

We've gotten really good at playing together. On a regular basis our family room transforms into a dance floor. We have family wrestling competitions, spontaneous games of tag, and charades. At the dinner table we play games like "We're going on a picnic" or "Two truths and a lie." Continually growing the fun makes everyone happy, because we are building on our strength.

A research and facilitation tool called Appreciative Inquiry suggests that noticing the good stuff is a practice that can benefit individuals and groups. According to the Appreciative Inquiry Commons:

> In its broadest focus, it involves systematic discovery of what gives "life" to a living system when it is most alive, most effective, and most constructively capable in economic, ecological, and human terms. [Appreciative Inquiry] involves, in a central way, the art and practice of asking questions that strengthen a system's capacity to apprehend, anticipate, and heighten positive potential.[1]

In a work setting, I've watched this approach transform leadership teams and inspire strategic planning efforts that never would have come from an older strategy of looking at the challenges first.

While I'm not suggesting Appreciative Inquiry is always the right strategy, it is something worth giving a try.

What is "the good stuff" in your life or your organization? How might you focus on these strengths, appreciate them, and help them to grow?

---

[1] "What is Appreciative Inquiry?" from "A Positive Revolution in Change: Appreciative Inquiry," David L. Cooperrider and Diana Whitney, Appreciative Inquiry Commons. Retrieved from http://appreciativeinquiry.case.edu/intro/whatisai.cfm

12 Treating People Well

At dinnertime when I was growing up there were usually seven to nine of us squeezed around the thick wooden table that my dad had made. Five kids, two parents, and usually a friend or neighbor. It was loud and busy with several conversations going on and someone shouting a request for chicken. My mom would shuttle back and forth from the oven to the table while we laughed and listened to stories from the day. My clearest memory, however, was of the stories my dad, the tree surgeon, told about his interactions with his customers.

He talked about Mrs. Prossor, who always invited him in for lemonade or a cup of coffee. Even though she lived in a mansion in Bergen County, New Jersey, she always took the time to chat with him about how his family was doing and the summer vacation spot they both liked. My dad spoke warmly of this client, and often raised the story as an illustration for us of how he expected us to treat others. He believed all people deserved to be treated with dignity, respect, and kindness whether they show up covered in sawdust and tree chemicals, as he often did, or dressed in their Sunday best.

He spoke of other clients with a seething resentment. Cursing and ranting about customers who treated him with disrespect, he showed us the pain and anger that could result from a person being treated poorly.

What I took away from those dinner table experiences was a commitment to treat people well. Whether they were rich and famous, down on their luck and on the street, or in some ordinary middle place. What I've found about this commitment, however, is that it is not always so easy to carry out.

When I'm exhausted or overextended, it's all too easy for me to be the one yelling at everyone in the house (in tones that embarrass even me). I've also noticed that when I'm scared, angry, or sad, the impulse to distance myself from other people tends to leave them feeling like they were not treated well. I see a direct relationship between how I feel about myself and how I treat others.

Sometimes mistreatment occurs though unintentional or oblivious actions. After college, I helped launch the Points of Light Foundation in Washington, DC. My job was to pilot a new youth fellowship and to hire young people in several states to work with me. For their first week of training, I flew the young people to DC, set them up in a hotel, and instructed them to meet me at the Foundation on the first day of the program.

What I didn't realize was that for two of the fellows, all young African American men who had grown up in low-income families, this trip was a major event. It was the first time they had traveled by plane or stayed in a hotel. When the hotel asked them for a credit card for a deposit, they had to admit they didn't have one. It was a time when showing up on time and looking good mattered a lot. So, when they were given inaccurate directions on a hot, DC morning on top of everything else, they responded with anger.

The young men felt they had not been treated well. And they were right. When they let me know how they felt, my eyes were opened to how easy it is for us to hurt one another when our backgrounds are different and we don't take the time to check out our assumptions about what other people know or don't know, and need or don't need. This was not the first time I'd learn this lesson, and it wouldn't be the last.

What does this issue of treating people well stir up in you? When have you not treated someone well? What was going on for you at that time?

13 Transitions

After I wrote my first book, which was about choices women make in their twenties, I began running workshops for women on the topic of transitions and change. I publicized the first workshop and anticipated walking into a room full of twenty-somethings. When I arrived, I noticed that women of all ages had shown up. A little daunted, and worried that I had nothing to offer women my mom's age and older, I began as best I could. The women talked about the transitions they were currently facing. Some were ending relationships, others were starting new jobs, and still others were coming to know different parts of themselves for the first time. I began to understand that change and transition are themes that reoccur throughout our lives.

In *Transitions: Making Sense of Life's Changes*, William Bridges outlines phases of transitions and makes a distinction between the external changes that happen to us, and the internal psychological transitions that accompany these external shifts. The book reminds me of the opportunities transitions allow, because they shake up our patterns.

We can make use of the times when things are in flux. For example, transitioning from one boss to another might be a good time to redefine the valuable assets that you bring to your organization. Moving from one school year to the next could be a great time to set new guidelines and routines.

At a recent work meeting I heard the story of a large, well-established medical school that had experienced a few years of decline and low morale. People throughout the school recognized that it was time for a change. The director, new to the school, seized the opportunity and asked, "What is needed to make this school the best it can be?" Rather than react from a place of fear, he used the moment to frame a question about possibility. In doing so, he helped the school embark on a path of positive transformation.

As external shifts occur, we have internal opportunities to grow, to get stronger, and to become clearer about our strengths and our goals. If we listen closely during these times, and participate consciously, these periods can be our most important teachers.

Are you in the midst of transition in some part of your life now? What do you notice about it? Can you use it to make an internal or external shift you desire?

14 Working with Conflict

Most organizations contain pockets of tension and conflict. Sometimes it's a manager who won't work with another manager. At other times a project has created gridlock between the project's leaders and management. Conflict can take a million different forms, but it's inherent in complex, human systems. The important questions are, how do people work with conflict as it emerges, and how can they use it productively to strengthen their own and the organization's capacities?

In graduate school I was introduced to a new way of thinking about conflict through Marshall Rosenberg's *Nonviolent Communication: A Language of Life.* According to Rosenberg in addition to resolving the conflict, it is useful to help people feel more openhearted and connected to each other. He describes a four-step process:

> First, we observe what is actually happening in
> a situation.... Next, we state how we feel when
> we observe this action.... Thirdly, we say what
> needs of ours are connected to the feelings we
> have identified.... And the fourth component
> [is] a very specific request.... This fourth com-
> ponent addresses what we are wanting from
> the other person that would enrich our lives.[1]

When I first encountered Rosenberg's work, I was navigating my way through a new marriage and trying to
feel at home in a house my husband purchased before he
met me. The walls were all light beige, and I happened
to be a color freak. I was very particular about the shade
of blue I wanted in the dining room, the lime green I
wanted in the office, and the cherry red I imagined on
one family room wall. In some rooms, my strong opin-
ions meshed nicely with my husband's, and our marriage
went along smoothly as coats of paint were applied and
furniture was rearranged. When we got to the family
room, however, we hit an impasse.

After weeks of no movement, and my growing anxiety
that this marriage would never work if we couldn't re-
solve the red wall conflict, I attempted to use the Nonviolent Communication (NVC) process. When my husband and I tried to make a decision about painting the
wall, he said he liked things as they were. As I examined
the feelings that emerged for me, I found frustration that

---

[1] Marshall B. Rosenberg, *Nonviolent Communication: A Language of
Life*, 2nd ed. (Encinitas, CA: PuddleDancer Press, 2003), 6.

I had to negotiate this simple decision, anxiety that my marriage would squash my creative impulses, and anger that I couldn't just do it my way and move on. Underneath these feelings I realized that I needed to feel more autonomy in my marriage. We had been negotiating a thousand collaborative decisions from what silverware we would put on our wedding registry to what we were going to do on Saturday night for dinner. I wanted more freedom to make this decision about the paint without his input or opinion. And I was willing to give him the same autonomy on other issues. As an artistic person, I felt the need to have a blank canvas, some paint, and no one looking over my shoulder.

Figuring out how to frame this request was not easy. Rosenberg suggests making a request that you think the other person can agree to. I realized I was willing to give up a lot to gain this autonomy, so I phrased the request like this: "If I gave you 100% creative power to make interior design decisions in the living room, would you be willing to give me the same in the family room?"

In the end, he was, and the red wall still stands. When I think back on it, going through the process not only got me the red wall, it strengthened our marriage. I learned how important autonomy and my creative process were to me, even in this new configuration of a marriage. I also learned that I was married to someone who was patient enough to work through a process like this, do his own reflection, and compromise so that we could both get our needs met.

Since that time I've used this process in many personal and professional settings, and it has worked. Fuming one day about an early morning work email, I arrived at my hairdresser's ready to send an antagonistic response to my colleague. My super-smart hairdresser, Ashley, slowed me down by asking what outcome I wanted from my email. Her question stopped me cold for a few minutes and helped me remember the NVC process. As a result, I talked through my feelings and needs with her and framed a positive request in the email. My colleague agreed to my request within minutes. What could have been a day full of conflict was resolved peacefully and productively.

Imagine a situation where you are aware of a conflict; can you imagine walking yourself through these steps? What other tools have you found to be helpful in dealing with conflict?

15 Right-Size Your Purpose

Yoga teacher and scholar Stephen Cope's book *The Great Work of Your Life* interprets the 2,000-year-old Bhagavad Gita for ordinary people who know little of the Hindu text. The heart of the book shows readers how to live more clearly into their calling and suggests that the deepest fulfillment in life comes from embarking on this journey.

Cope quotes Thomas Merton, who was writing in the masculine style of his time:

> Every man has a vocation to be someone: but he must understand clearly that in order to fulfill this vocation he can only be one person: himself.[1]

---

[1] Stephen Cope, *The Great Work of Your Life: A Guide for the Journey to Your True Calling* (New York: Bantam Books/Random House, Inc., 2012), 23.

This quote speaks to the idea that while there is a universal invitation to find our purpose as humans, for each of us there is a very specific, idiosyncratic version of what it means to be ourselves.

The book notes that sometimes our work needs to be downsized so that we can achieve our vocation. Cope tells the story of Henry David Thoreau, who moved to New York to try to become a writer in the fast-paced literary world of his time. Cope reports, "His work was mediocre—and widely disregarded." Thoreau returned home feeling a failure and wrote, "Be humbly who you are."[2]

"Thoreau now saw clearly that the journey of a writer was not the outer journey to New York, but the inner journey to his own voice."[3] From the tiny cabin he built upon his return from the big city and his big ambitions, he "right-sized" his image of his work in the world, creating the work that made him one of America's greatest writers.

This story spoke to me because too often I come up with ideas that are much too big to make happen. When I first began thinking about writing this book, I imagined creating a weighty, many-hundred-page tome. Every time I thought about working on it, I felt both pulled by a deep call to write it and hopeless about finding the time that

---

[2] Ibid., 41–42.
[3] Ibid., 45.

I imagined it would require. But then, shortly after reading of Thoreau's journey to "right-sizing" his purpose, another book arrived in my mailbox, a small book with lots of white space on every page. A light bulb went off in my head. This I could do, I could write a small book.

With that vision, my writing took off. I started spending little chunks of time here and there working on it, and felt invigorated and free. Before long, I had a draft. The right-sizing was just what I needed to put my vision into action.

Is there something big you would like to do someday, but it feels a bit out of reach? What happens if you shrink the idea down to something that feels more doable?

16 What Moves You?

I can't pick up one of Kelly Corrigan's books without crying. I feel so much resonance between the stories she writes about being a mom and how I feel about parenting my own children that I can't read her writing without feeling cracked open. She helps me to experience a deeper level of whatever I'm facing in my own life that day.

This theme is not about knowing or liking Corrigan's work. What matters is that her writing is one of the things that moves me. For my husband, some singer-songwriters stir his soul. Put on Jackson Browne or David Bromberg or some other less known folk musicians and you will lose him for a little while to his own world. He will be busy being moved.

Last time I visited my good friend Arrington, I was feeling hopeless about finding the spiritual community and support that I was craving. She's a beacon of faith and creator of devotional spaces, so I knew just being with her would feed me. What I didn't know was how moved I would be by the simple vases of flowers that I found all over her apartment.

When I sat in her meditation room, there was a vase on the altar with a single tulip. On the kitchen table the rest of the tulips sat in a pewter vase. When I woke up in the morning on the couch, dead ahead on top of the TV was another vase with a collection of roses. The morning before I left I sat, staring at the vase on top of the TV, and opened myself to the depth of my desire for more support in my spiritual journey. I soaked in the love I felt being in my friend's apartment and noticed again the beauty of the flowers before me.

Before I left, I vowed to start buying flowers each week and surrounding myself with the simple beauty and support I felt in Arrington's home. While there was no guarantee that what moved me that weekend would have that same effect at home, it was a place to start.

For each of us, various authors, musicians, or objects capture themes and nuances that stir us and open us to new ways.

What opens you up and makes you more of the person you want to be? Can you get some of it in your life today?

17 What's Your Vice?

It is amazing how many people I know who have complicated relationships to eating or drinking. For me, this complication shows up in my love for sweets—from Jolly Rancher hard candies to creme-filled treats like Twinkies, Yodels, and Oreos. While my struggle has not been clinically diagnosed, it regularly gets in the way of my attempts to be my best self.

I've spent years watching this addiction and trying to control it by playing around with my behaviors. I have restrained myself from sugar for years at a time. I've meditated on the experience of craving. I've let myself binge without remorse. I've read books about the cycle of addiction and tried to notice its emotional patterns. I've gotten help from Eastern medicine practitioners in an attempt to balance the systems in my body so the cravings are not so strong. Over time I've learned a lot, and I have shifted some significant patterns.

Unfortunately, though, all my learning doesn't keep me from tossing Skittles in my mouth as I write this. Right now I'm letting myself eat sugar when I want to while I watch the connection in my mind and body between sitting down to "hard work" and indulging in the helpful little drugs of sugar and caffeine, which seem to make the hard work easier. For the moment I've decided that I'm getting so much joy and satisfaction from accomplishing the hard work that it overpowers both the bad physical feelings I have after eating too much sugar, and the impatience I develop with everyone around me when I eat sugar or drink caffeine.

I don't think this experiment will last. Eventually, I'm pretty sure, I will want to feel better both physically and emotionally, and I'll give up sugar for a while again.

In *Women, Food and God*, Geneen Roth shares her philosophy that "our relationship to food is an exact microcosm of our relationship to life itself."[1] According to Roth, if we are starving for spiritual food, then perhaps we habitually overeat, trying to fill the emptiness with hamburgers. If we believe we are not loved, we might diet on and off in an effort to win the love we are seeking. In the retreats she runs, Roth gives talks, teaches meditation, and has people sit in front of their food, being present with it for quite a long time before they eat. The process sounds like one I could really use right about now. But at the end of her book, she reminds

---

[1] Geneen Roth, *Women, Food and God: An Unexpected Path to Almost Everything* (New York: Scribner, 2010), 2.

readers what I try to remember myself: "Real change comes bit by bit. It takes great effort to become effort-less at anything. There are no quick fixes."[2] Roth's ideas have given me encouragement to be more curious about why, for example, I'm grabbing for yet another Skittle.

What's your relationship to food or alcohol? Can you be curious, instead of judgmental, about it? Does it have anything to do with other needs that might be emotional or spiritual?

---

[2] Ibid., 197.

18 Get Out the Watercolors

One day, I was home from work with sick kids and feeling frustrated. It was ten o'clock in the morning, and I had already played board games, washed dishes, and served snacks. I searched my mind for something that might bring the day alive for me and entertain the kids at the same time. The words "get out the watercolors" popped into my head.

With that I marched over to the art supply box and riffled through until I came up with a well-used pack of Crayola watercolors and some paper. After I spread them out on the kitchen table, my kids and I began to paint. They busied themselves with broad brushes of pink and green. I painted a list of themes for me to think about in the coming weeks. Within minutes a tired, boring day turned into one that was full of life.

While pushing a stroller later that day I wondered, "How is this theme, 'Get Out the Watercolors,' relevant in the workplace?" I remembered a party for my friend Lisa's new book, *Moments of Impact: How to Design Strategic Conversations That Accelerate Change*. During the party, business school students demonstrated how a team could create a visual image of their entire business plan on one sheet of newsprint. Looking at the newsprint was a lot more fun than reading a ten-page plan.

Meetings can be deadly. Too many meetings fail to maximize the connections or the creativity in the room. In low-energy meetings, it's often not even clear whether anything is getting done. Even with talented people in the room, a group can keep rehearsing the same scripts and producing the same mediocre work. "Get out the watercolors" in a business context would challenge us to use more creative formats, agendas, and physical materials during meetings.

In Boston some years ago, I attended a training on coaching offered by a group called Interaction Associates. They had us sit back to back with partners while instructing each other how to create a playdough object that we conjured with our minds. This exercise was designed to demonstrate that in coaching you can't just tell your client what to do. You have to think about what the other person is seeing and experiencing and attempt to make suggestions that will work for them, rather than for you. Inserting new materials into the process can often make activities feel fresh and help people open up to the tasks in front of them, whether they are corporate executives or preschoolers.

On that morning with my sick kids, getting out the watercolors brought me to life. It opened the door for me to be creatively engaged, and on that day, it was just what I needed.

What is your relationship to creative materials? Do you surround yourself with any either at home or at work? What's one creative material you can get and use this week?

19 Connecting with Nature

Sitting on the edge of the San Francisco Bay one New Year's Day I felt so peaceful. The sun was bright and the surface of the water was sparkling. I sat inside my parked car while Ellie (my two-year-old) napped in the backseat while I wrote my intentions for the new year: blog once a week, invest some money in my coaching firm, keep working to establish a good rhythm in my home, take those financial steps Noel and I keep talking about, and keep protecting Sundays for family time.

After a few minutes, I glanced up and noticed the reflections on the water again. I noticed the seagulls and that my chest felt as open as the vista in front of me. I began to wonder what it was about the water that made me feel this way. I thought about other places that create a sense of peace. Somewhere down this river of thoughts it occurred to me that this year, instead of listing the things I want to accomplish, I could name the places I want to be more often. Research suggests that being in certain spaces almost always leads to positive outcomes:

> Even three to five minutes of contact with nature can significantly reduce stress and have a complex impact on emotions, reducing anger and fear and increasing pleasant feelings.[1]

I've seen this with my son. Kids need to be in nature as much, if not more, than we do. I've known since Will was a toddler that if I'm having a challenging day with him, all I need to do is get to a park. Once we are out in the fresh air and there's room to run, everything gets better.

I learned to value nature when I was young. My dad was a tree surgeon and after a long day of work, he retreated to his garden. There he could let go of the stress of the day. Having access to lots of land growing up, my brothers and I were often out exploring the woods, pulling up vegetables, or playing kickball with friends. Family adventures usually involved a state park, a farm, or the beach.

Many people would agree: the idea that connecting with nature brings out the best in us is a no-brainer. The trick is to act on this knowledge and build our routines and habits around it. Deciding to walk to school or work

---

[1] "What Impact Does the Environment Have on Us?" Taking Charge of Your Health & Wellbeing, Center for Spirituality and Healing and Charlson Meadows, University of Minnesota. Retrieved from http://www.takingcharge.csh.umn.edu/explore-healing-practices/healing-environment/what-impact-does-environment-have-us

once a week, spending some portion of the weekend hiking, or finding a natural spot your work team can go—these all take effort and planning. If we can just remember how great it feels to connect to the natural world, our everyday routines might run more smoothly than they do today.

What benefit do you notice for yourself, your family, or work-group when you connect to the natural world? How can you connect with nature today or this week?

20 The Nonlinear Path

I have had a bit of an obsession lately with tablecloths. Not so much that I have to have them on the table, but my imagination is taking off with the concept and possibility in them. The other day I had one free hour and was restless. Like a little rat in a cage, I drove down one street, then another, asking myself, "What do I want to do? Stop for some tea? Buy art supplies? Go shopping? Get an errand done? Stop my car right now and write for a few minutes?" As my mind darted from one idea to the next, my car drove me to my favorite fabric store: Stone Mountain Daughters in Berkeley.

I put money in the meter for my remaining forty-five minutes of freedom and entered the store. As I walked aimlessly from aisle to aisle, I took note of patterns and colors. What am I looking for? Did I want to make a gift for someone? (No, I always do that; I want to do something for me.) But I didn't need anything. Who cares if you don't need anything; make something cool and fun for yourself. But I couldn't think of anything I wanted to make. Every minute or two I almost shouted at myself, "Hurry up, this is your time, don't waste it." I kept hitting the same stumbling block. I couldn't buy material if I didn't know what it was for. But try as I might, I couldn't land on the right project.

With ten minutes left on my meter, I decided that because life is short and I might not get myself back to this store for another six months, I had better seize the moment. I picked four fabrics that I thought worked well together, paid my $23.14, and returned to my car so I could scurry back to pick up my daughter for lunch.

Back home, the material just sat—first in my office, then in my dining room, then in my bedroom. Every couple of days I picked it up and admired it. I absolutely *love* fabric, and the ones I picked were perfect. Perfect for something. All cotton; one was a dark purple with circles and designs inside the circles. Another was a lime green with maroon polka dots. A third was a mix of pink and lime green, and the last one was white with an unusual texture. Together, they were perfect for something.

A month later, I got the sewing machine out and balanced the fabric on top of it. I still didn't know what I was going to create, but that was a step forward. A couple of nights later, the ah-ha moment came.

Around the same time, I was brainstorming the future of my work with two friends. I sketched out the elements of support that I felt most women needed to reach their goals. Some needed a coach. Others needed information. But a third, and significant group, needed other women. Other women who face similar challenges, have similar aspirations, or are simply willing to be honest with each other. I thought, to create the right environment for women to connect you need a table. Most likely a kitchen table to sit around, to share stories, to eat or drink, to witness grief and anxiety, to help each other give birth to the dreams and aspirations that have been hiding under the covers.

All of the sudden, my material picking and tablecloth obsessing made sense. I was feeling called to create a space for women to gather, and that calls for a beautiful cloth. The next morning, I woke early and pieced together a tablecloth to remind me how important gathering women is to my work in the world.

Can you let yourself follow a whim or a random idea without knowing where it might take you? Have you done this before? If so, where did it lead?

21 The Hard Stuff

When I was living in Washington, DC, and then later working with teens in Boston, I frequently heard news of local violence. An assault and robbery in the neighborhood, a toddler injured by a gunshot, or the yells of the woman next door would rattle me and send me into rage, grief, or anxiety. These events unearthed me, in part because I was so close to them. They were happening where I lived, or to the friends of children I loved, or in a city I was deeply committed to. I was also deeply affected by these events, because I had the emotional capacity to let them in. I had a strong support network that helped me process my feelings. Once processed, the feelings became fuel for passionate speeches I gave about the need for young people's involvement in community action.

In recent years I've been further removed from urban violence, and in some ways more protected emotionally from letting its impact in. There is so much of it, and I feel so powerless over it. It is easier to walk along my suburban streets and ignore what I know is happening over the hills in Oakland. It's harder to close off to the random suburban violence that occurs in towns that look just like mine even when they are far away. Currently, that's the news that is more likely to rock my world. When I have the emotional space and time to let in the hard news about violence, it connects me to a deep vulnerability I feel as a human and a parent, and to the powerlessness that accompanies it.

It also makes me ask, "How do we stay present to the most difficult aspects of life?"

When the really hard stuff happens—a death, an act of violence against someone you know, a serious injury, a divorce, the discovery of a childhood trauma or abuse— what do we do in response?

Being present with these challenges is perhaps our hardest work. They remind us of our vulnerability, our lack of control, and our pain. We so often run from the feelings and sensations brought on by difficult situations for good reasons. Who wants to feel the ache of grief when it can be numbed with a shot of Johnnie Walker? Or experience anger and resentment when escaping into a shopping mall might distract us? Why would we choose to face how vulnerable and powerless we are?

While writing *Seven Thousand Ways to Listen*, Mark Nepo was losing his hearing and trying to make sense of what that meant for his life. He writes:

> Every disturbance, whether resolved or not,
> is making space for an inner engagement. As
> a shovel digs up and displaces earth in a way
> that must seem violent to the earth, an interior
> space is revealed for the digging. In just this
> way, when experience opens us, it often feels
> violent and the urge, quite naturally, is to refill
> that opening, to make it the way it was. But ev-
> ery experience excavates a depth, which reveals
> its wisdom once opened to the air.[1]

This quote reminds me of the strength and resiliency that can emerge if we are willing not to run.

The women I met while teaching yoga in a residential detox program modeled this ability for me. Before each yoga class, they gathered in a circle and shared stories about what they were feeling that day, finishing with a prayer for strength and thankfulness. Week after week, I listened as they opened up about being sexually abused, physically abused, or being offered drugs when they were just children. Some weeks they were dying for drugs or a drink, other weeks they were filled with gratitude for being clean and having a second chance in life. As I heard their stories, I was in awe of the inner strength they exhibited.

Their resilience and ability to be with the hard stuff encouraged me to stay present whenever negative emotions surfaced in me. Though I might prefer to eat something

---

[1] Mark Nepo, *Seven Thousand Ways to Listen: Staying Close to What Is Sacred* (New York: Free Press, 2012), 6.

sugary or look for another distraction, I worked hard to face my own feelings. When I can stick with my own feelings, sometimes they will shift, and I will feel a remarkable sense of calm and peace. The more I stay present to the hard stuff coming up in my life, the more I can rest, connect with others, and sustain my creative work.

What is hard or challenging in your life today? Is your tendency to stay present to it, or to run from it? What might support you to stay present to it, if only for a moment?

22 Attend to the Foundation

For many years, I was a raving workaholic. I loved my work, and I lived my work eighty hours a week. On the surface it was exciting and ego-gratifying, but on a deeper level, the rigorous schedule made me tired, lonely, and depressed. It took a major health crisis to wake me up and help me realize that my health and desire for closer relationships mattered more than the work.

This is a fairly common story. People are cruising along in a fast-paced life when some health, financial, or family issue rears up to interrupt the momentum. After such an abrupt stop, people may notice that something more important in their life needs attention. In my case, I could avoid noticing my significant anxiety when I was moving so fast. As I slowed down, I began to see that to be healthier and happier, I had to dig in and investigate the issues causing the anxiety.

In my coaching practice, I often notice a disconnect between a client's larger, spoken desires and his or her basic but unspoken needs. For example, one woman who came to me wanted to write a book. But her workspace was a disaster, and she was regularly overtired. All of her attempts to create a consistent writing practice had fallen short. Another client wanted to raise a large sum of money to start a new venture. She had bold plans, but she was always worried about money and had trouble paying her rent.

On a societal level, the acceleration of change and a variety of other influences have landed us in an unhealthy state. Many adults face one health issue or another, ranging from eating challenges, to sleep challenges, to mental health and heart issues. Our kids face similar issues. Our children's future viewed through the trends in diabetes, suicide, anxiety, gun violence, and obesity should be enough to wake us up to the reality that as a society, we are not well.

Tending to the foundation means that in order to make progress on our aspirations, we have got to take stock and pay attention to our basic needs. If you want to write a book but you are always too tired when you sit down to the computer, then spend a couple of weeks going to sleep at a reasonable hour every night. When you are more rested, begin your writing practice. As a society, if we want the next generation to flourish, we've got to take seriously the physical and mental health issues our children are facing.

Are there health or other foundation issues in your life that need attention? If so, how might ignoring them be getting in the way of other goals or interests you have?

23 The Power of Culture

I once worked in an organization that was obsessed with its organizational culture. Once hired you were expected to learn the mission, core values, and a host of founding stories that all carried forward the messages of that culture. Much like in the military, the culture permeated the design of the uniform, the rules for walking down the street, and protocols for meetings that involved checking in and appreciating the organization's positive impact. In my orientation, the CEO told me to withhold judgment of the organization until I had lived within it for at least a year. Initially, I resisted this advice. But what I learned over time was that there was a lot of wisdom to what he said. To really understand a culture, sometimes you have to let yourself fully participate.

From the inside you can understand much more about why things are done the way they are and perhaps reap some of the benefits. You can also develop a sounder base from which to reflect upon and critique the organization.

The leaders of many companies and institutions invest time and money in developing a healthy organizational culture. Those who do, know it can have a big payoff. The same is true of the effort required to develop a healthy, positive culture in a family.

In my own family, I have tried to create a culture in which we actively value family time. There are so many outside demands on our time during the week as we race from school to work to baseball, dance class, and social events. It takes real effort to carve out time for family and to structure it in a way that works for everyone.

For us, Sunday is Family Day. On Sundays we avoid spending time with our electronic devices so that we can spend time together, preferably out in nature. For several years we attended church, but after a while we realized that it did not provide the feeling of connection and togetherness that we all craved. I miss church, because it feeds me spiritually. But right now, creating positive family time is more important. So we go hiking, we take picnics to a park, we hang out at home playing board games, or we visit with friends the whole family can enjoy. On Sunday night, we have grounding time, our homemade version of church that keeps the thread of spirituality alive and reinforces our connection with each other.

In my coaching practice, I also like to encourage others to cultivate relationship-focused cultures. At the beginning of a group meeting with clients, we take time to check in. Rather than rush through this part, we allocate enough time to hear what's really going on in our lives. Only then do we move to the task list and agenda. These check-ins often help me to notice issues I need to focus on in my life as well as in my work. Having a culture that values this sharing seems to make the sharing deeper and more meaningful.

When we take the time to establish a strong and supportive culture, in our work settings and at home, we make space for the members to grow and thrive.

Think of a group you are a part of at work, at home, or in your community. What values does this subculture emphasize, and what practices support these values?

24 Fresh Starts and Strong Finishes

When I ran a nonprofit youth organization in Boston, my team and I repainted the office walls three times in four years. Every time it was an attempt at a fresh start. Each time the youth and adult staff chose colors, made a plan, and dove into a weeklong process of clearing shelves, taping windows, and applying a fresh coat of paint. The process improved team morale, office cleanliness, and clarity of direction for the organization. It became a ritual of sorts that helped us get excited about our work and aligned with our goals for the year.

I go through a similar cleansing and refreshing process in my house at the beginning of each school year. I challenge my kids to empty kitchen cabinets, the refrigerator, and the freezer before I buy more food. I take bins of toys out of their room and put them down in the basement for rainy days when they sort and rediscover them. I move pictures around walls, furniture around rooms, and change rugs with other old ones I've stored in the basement, all in an attempt to give rooms a new look. In response to all my spontaneous rearranging, my husband and I end up talking about what the family needs in the year to come. The process invigorates me and gives me hope for what's to come in the fall and beyond. Beginnings are my thing.

A former boss saw my love for beginnings and also noticed that I was not as good in the middle or the finish of things. This insight enabled him to pull me aside near the end of an important project when I was getting lazy and starting to checkout. He encouraged me to finish the training event strong by nailing all the logistical details, putting my heart into the closing content, doing a thorough debrief with the team, and using the finish to plant seeds for activities that could ripple out beyond the event.

While it didn't come naturally or easily, I followed his advice and found the results extremely powerful. The project finished with a great result, and the staff involved left knowledgeable and inspired for their next projects. The lesson I took away is that finishing strong matters just as much as starting strong. And I've kept relearning the lesson in different areas of my life.

Sticking with things in the middle is my next challenge.

What part of any process do you like most—the beginning, the middle, or the end? Do you see patterns in your behavior as you relate to these phases? Can you imagine doing something differently this week and focusing a bit more on a phase that you usually neglect?

25 The Wisdom of Trees

I love trees. The one I'm looking at now worries little about the winds that will come, the pine needles it will loose, or the growth of its roots. It just stands there outside my dining room window reminding me that it's okay if I don't know how my life will turn out.

By contrast, when I observe my mind, all I hear are messages of worry. I wonder: "What will happen at the meeting next week? Am I going to succeed with the new work project? How much time is too much to spend at work when the kids are still so young? How am I going to finish this writing and get dinner on the table by five o'clock?"

The tree tells me to trust. Staring at it reminds my lungs to take a deep breath and my mind to have faith that these questions will get answered in their own time.

Noticing this, I find it easy to see why so many people turn to nature when they want greater calm or are struggling with big issues in their lives. The feelings inspired by looking at the tree allow me to place my attention on the idea of trusting the unknown, rather than the swirl of anxiety.

In *The Art of Changing the Brain*, author James Zull helps readers to see that our brains are in a constant state of discernment over where to place our attention. Should I go with the feelings of anxiety about all those unanswered questions? Or should my brain be pulled toward the thought that focusing on the tree brings to mind, "Relax, these questions will be answered in their due time."

Zull writes:

> Feelings become especially distracting when
> we really care about the answer to a problem.
> If the answer is important to us, our feelings
> become distracting.[1]

He goes on to state:

> If self-discipline is to work, we must care about
> discipline more than the other things that vie
> for our attention. We can achieve discipline [or

---

[1] James E. Zull, *The Art of Changing the Brain: Enriching the Practice of Teaching by Exploring the Biology of Learning* (Sterling, VA: Stylus Publishing, LLC, 2002), 75.

in my case, relaxing about the unknown] when
we *feel* that discipline is what we want the
most.[2]

With repeated experiments I have witnessed that the
way of trust yields so much more than the way of worry.
With a million unknowns in my future, I'd better stay
close to that tree.

*Ask yourself: in what ways am I living in the unknown right
now? How does it feel? And, what might help me to relax with
it?*

---

[2] Ibid., 76.

26 Let Life Change You

When I was growing up, my dad was a very hard-working guy, running a tree service business and keeping food on the table for our family of seven. He was out the door by 5:30 every morning and exhausted when he came in at 5:00 every night. As a result, I didn't have a lot of contact with him. When I did see him, my impression was that he was a really strong man, complete with cannonball muscles in his arms that we would hang on as he pulled us up in the air. Even though he had fallen out of a tree and crushed most of the bones in his legs a few years earlier, we never thought about him as a man with any weak points. He recovered from that fall with as much strength and grace as he had done anything. I never saw him show vulnerability until the day my younger brother was in a terrible car accident.

I was the first person to be notified about the accident because my brother and I were traveling together in California. We had flown from the East Coast a week before to spend spring break driving from Napa Valley to Los Angeles. He had dropped me off the day before the accident at a student leadership conference at UCLA and driven to San Diego without me. Later that day he fell asleep at the wheel and his car flipped over. He was in critical condition several hours south when I got the call. Immediately, friends from the conference gathered around to offer support. My two closest friends urged me to let them come with me to the hospital. I told them I was fine and drove by myself to the hospital all the while imagining dozens of worse case scenarios. I will never forget the feeling in my body as I walked into his hospital room. His body was covered in tubes, and it was unclear if he was dead or alive. As rapidly as I walked in, I walked right back out into the hallway and crumpled against the wall. I was far from home, alone, and terrified of losing my brother.

Twenty-four hours later, I left to go back to college on the East Coast. That same day, my parents arrived from the East Coast to care for my brother while he began to recover, transitioning out of intensive care to a regular room, and eventually to a state in which he could handle the plane ride back East. During the rest of that spring, my parents cared for him as he healed from a punc-tured liver and multiple internal injuries. Meanwhile, I finished the semester at school in Virginia. It was June before I saw my brother or my parents.

My brother, while still healing physically, seemed like the same old Brendan. My father, however, appeared to be a changed man. When he said grace my first night back from school, there were tears in his eyes as he expressed gratitude for Brendan's recovery and my return from school. This experience happened repeatedly throughout the month and for the rest of his life. It seemed that the accident had rocked his world so completely that he could no longer keep up the façade of impenetrable strength. As a result he began to let the world in to see his humanness on a whole new level.

While I realized that day in the hospital that I should have let my friends in, only years later did I begin to let the lesson sink in. It took a health crisis of my own to crack me open and help me to see that it is okay to need people, to let them in, and to show my weaker parts.

I learned through my dad's example and my own experience that we can allow events—whether they are dramatic and tragic, or subtle and exciting—to change us in powerful and healing ways.

What has changed you? Can you tell the story and allow it to continue to deepen its impact?

27 **The Power of Presence**

When my son was in second grade, our mornings often began with conflict. He didn't want to brush his hair, finish his homework, or walk to school. I wanted him to do all those things. He would yell, I would yell back. One of us would storm off, but somehow, by 8:05 a.m., we managed to get out the door. On most days, when we walked back into the house at two o'clock, the struggle would continue.

After one particularly volatile morning, I made a mental note that I wanted to change our pattern. I spent the day going about my usual paid and unpaid work. A few minutes before he was to arrive home, I stopped myself, realizing that how I greeted him as he returned from his school day was the thing that mattered most. I sat down by the window and stared out at the neighbor's house. As I sat, I began thinking about the power of being waited for. A memory of my grandma sitting in her room waiting for me to come home from school when I was in elementary school came to mind. Another memory floated in of my best friend sitting by my side when I was really sick. Every time I opened my eyes I saw a lit candle and her sitting nearby. Both of these memories evoked a deep feeling of being cared for.

When the carpool pulled up, I watched Will closely as he climbed out the back door, threw his backpack over his right shoulder, and ran to the door. I opened it before he reached for it and welcomed him in with a giant hug, pouring love into his little body. The rest of the day was filled with harmony and sweetness. This attention seemed to be just what he needed to settle back into his life at home.

I've always been moved by the power of people's presence. I feel the power of an older mentor's presence when I sit down for breakfast with him and immediately slow down. Mel doesn't need to say a word. His attention speaks volumes. His warmth shines through and invites my heart to open. His eyes tell me that he is glad I'm there and doing the work I'm doing.

Cultivating this level of presence is not always easy. In the book *Presence: Human Purpose and the Field of the Future*, the authors, who are innovators in the management field, break down the process necessary to break into new levels of innovation, creativity, and possibilities for our organizations. They state:

> We first thought of presence as being fully
> conscious and aware in the present moment.

Then we began to appreciate presence as deep listening, of being open beyond one's preconceptions and historical ways of making sense.... Ultimately, we came to see all these aspects of presence as leading to a state of "letting come," of consciously participating in a larger field of change. When this happens, the field shifts, and the forces shaping a situation can shift from re-creating the past to manifesting or realizing an emerging future.[1]

What comes to mind when you think about the power of presence? What is the quality of your presence right now? Is there something you can do today to deepen your attention to the present moment or let go of old ways of making sense of things?

---

[1] P. Senge, C. Scharmer, J. Jaworski, and B. Flowers, *Presence: Human Purpose and the Field of the Future* (Cambridge, MA: The Society for Organizational Learning, 2004), 11–12.

28 The Little Things

On Valentine's Day a couple of years ago, I drove to the airport with my two kids, Will and Ellie, to pick up my husband Noel. He was returning from a trip he had made to say goodbye to his dad, who was dying of cancer. I was feeling grateful, the way it is easy to feel grateful when someone is dying and you remember that every day is a gift. It had been a lucky morning on the child front. Ellie woke up at 5:50 a.m., instead of her usual 5:00—and she had been happy all morning, cooing and squealing in her bouncy seat in the kitchen. The easy morning gave me just enough time to make my mom's famous chocolate sauce as a Valentine's Day present for Noel.

I usually make the sauce at Christmas, because it's the thing I make that Noel loves the most. It's made with unsweetened chocolate squares (that are now hard to find in the grocery store), a boatload of sugar, a little milk, and a little cream. Noel cherishes his jar, making it last most of the year. He eats it late at night with ice cream and peanuts.

That Christmas, we had been sleep deprived and over-whelmed caring for a difficult infant and a young child, so I put making the chocolate sauce on the list of things to do once we regained some balance. Also on the list were buying or making Christmas gifts for friends, host-ing a holiday party, clipping my fingernails, and dying my hair. At that point I was still buying my older child, Will, school lunches everyday because preparing them at home was more than I could handle. Friends were still dropping off prepared meals for dinner, because they could tell we needed the support. While making the sauce was impossible that Christmas, the idea of making it lingered for weeks.

As we sat waiting by the gate at the airport, Will rested his head on my knee. Ellie shifted from nursing to sitting on my lap, looking out at all the people in the security line. We were a sweet little family pile, and I savored every minute of it. The five months since Ellie's birth had been incredibly challenging. No sleep, tons of crying, a bunch of anxiety for me, a tsunami of anger and power struggles from Will. It made unexpected gifts of these peaceful moments with my little ones.

People have told me that when someone close to them dies, "it's the little things" they miss the most. The way someone handed them the phone or made chicken pot pies. The notes they left out on the counter, or the way they laughed out loud at a family dinner. It makes so much sense to me that those are the things we want to hold onto, because they are the threads woven all through the days and nights we spend together. It's not the one shiny piece of gold fabric sewn on the quilt we miss; it's the simple repeated pattern.

On that Valentine's Day, it was the little things of making chocolate sauce and snuggling with my kids that filled my heart with gratitude and helped to put my challenging daily routine into perspective.

What's a little thing that matters to you today? How might you fit it into your day and savor it?

29 Rhythm

When Will was just three months old, I took him to the Japanese-Buddhist Foundation where I had been working before he was born. In the days preceding the visit, I was tired and weary from his newborn nighttime feeding schedule and still sorting through a lot of confusion about where to put my energy as a young parent. I felt overwhelmed by people's suggestions and book recommendations. Some suggested it was essential for me to eat only organic food and play classical music. Others warned me to make sure he was getting enough outside time, daily massage, and a myriad of other types of stimulation to ensure proper brain development.

My client at the time was the father of two young children. When he suggested that the daily rhythm in a home and in a child's life was one of the most important things to pay attention to, it resonated. And, it felt doable. Putting my focus on a routine that provided a consistent pattern of activity, food, and quiet allowed me to feel that I could grow into this new role of mom.

According to Merriam Webster, rhythm is "a regular, repeated pattern of sounds or movements."[1] When this idea is applied to the life of a baby, it can include anything from waking up, taking naps, and going to sleep at the same time everyday, to singing the same song when you prepare to transition into the car. This sense of life having a pattern allows babies and children to trust in what's happening around them.

It also helps adults. Not just at home, but in the workplace as well. When I am most productive, there is a consistent and healthy rhythm to my activities. I first get up and out for exercise, then sit down to a cup of tea, followed by a two-hour block of focused work and then a midday meal. When this pattern is well established, I find I produce more significant work, because I've been practicing settling in and focusing at the same time day after day.

Rhythm is also relevant to organizations. I try to pay attention to the pace of activities and if there is any built-in breathing room for employees in between big events or campaigns. When there is not, that has a price. This go, go, go rhythm often leads to burnout, loss of creativity, and decreasing excitement for the work.

---

[1] "rhythm." Merriam-Webster.com. Retrieved from http://www.merriam-webster.com

When I was a young parent, many aspects of our life improved if I turned my attention to the rhythm in our days. In organizational settings we do not often talk about rhythm, but I suspect it would have a similar impact.

How much attention do you give to the concept of rhythm in your home or workplace? What rhythm might help you to sustain your commitments, your creativity, and your energy?

30 How It Was Supposed to Be

One year I went through a phase of noticing just how different my life is from the ones I had imagined living.

There was the life in which I lived in Boston next door to my best friend, where, along with our partners, we raised kids in a communal spirit, had regular musical potlucks in our homes, and shared clothes like high schoolers even after we had turned forty. Loneliness was never an issue; my house was yellow and I never lacked for hipness.

Then there was the version of my life in which I lived with my family in a college-owned apartment on a small campus in Amherst, Massachusetts. I imagined an open green where the kids ate ice cream on warm summer nights and cute locally owned shops lined the streets of the commercial district. Again, I imagined a hustle and bustle in and out of my family's home as students took care of my kids, and friends dropped by for meals and conversation about community issues. In this version of life I had a giant computer screen, an office window with a great view, and tons of writing time.

There were several other versions, and in my fantasies all of them seemed more interesting, fulfilling, and connected than my current life. While I could see threads of these scenarios in my real life, the distance between what I had imagined and what was real seemed huge. Sitting with the reality of these gaps and my unhappiness about them is what finally moved me into action.

For a couple of months I grieved things I had been unwilling to grieve. For six or seven years I had clung to the notion that my husband and I were going to find a way to move back East where I could start working on those imaginary lives. Slowly, as I began to let go of this dream, I started saying good-bye to these imagined scenarios of "how it was supposed to be." And as I let go, I found new energy to build my present world.

That's when I started hosting a group of moms to discuss parenting and sent out an invitation for an open mic night of music in our home. I moved my workspace from a cramped office to the dining room where I had a giant window and view of the evergreens. I started appreciating the town commons where my kids already played. I reached out to my best friend in Boston and let her know how much I wanted to arrange regular summer visits and consistent contact with her.

A few months later I realized that I had made similar assumptions in my professional world. Even as I clung to ideas I had about how my work was going to spring to life, I began to notice the ways it was not happening. I imagined a new college program to help young adults clarify their sense of purpose and their authentic leadership. But the foundation I thought would fund it rejected my request for support. I wanted a thriving individual coaching practice. But when I began doing the marketing work to grow my practice, I realized I didn't have enough energy for marketing and coaching while I was raising small children. One after another, doors shut. Opportunities I expected to materialize didn't. Again, I was forced to let go of ideas and images I had of the future.

But, after a particularly clarifying conversation with an old client, I realized that the more I let go of the way I thought things were supposed to be, the more I could focus on whatever was in front of me. I began to notice how much I liked working part-time for the local college.

Looking back, I wish I could have let go sooner and allowed the flow of new relationships and opportunities to begin even sooner than they did.

Do you have ideas of how life or work should be that don't mesh with your current reality? How does it feel to think about these ideas? Can you notice how you might benefit by letting go of an idea that you are still holding onto?

31 Drop the Anger

As a young person, I was overwhelmed by feelings of powerlessness at having too little impact on my world. I learned that the best thing to do with anger was to stuff it down and eat some ice cream. As a result, I internalized the pattern of pushing anger down and moving on.

Having a child who also has lots of anger helped me to see that my early-life technique had limits. Some days, my reactions to my son were too big and too fast for me to stuff. I knew if I didn't want to hurt him or spend my days yelling, I had to learn a new way. Running helped, and so did giving myself "time-outs" when I felt the loss of control coming on full force. But sometimes, even those things weren't enough.

One day I read a hilarious article critiquing the advice often given to couples to never go to bed angry. In contrast, this author suggested that many fights could be diverted if people would just turn over and get some sleep. As an exhausted parent, I could get behind this kind of advice. Too often my husband and I would begin a late night fight and end up cracking up when one of us noticed we were fighting over something completely ridiculous because neither of us had slept in a week.

The article was a good reminder that there is a direct connection between where we are physically and how we show up emotionally. One of the things I love about parenting is seeing this connection between the physical and the emotional so directly. Get on the wrong side of a toddler who hasn't eaten all morning, and you know you are in big trouble. He will kick, scream, resist, and be completely irrational until he eats a bagel; within five minutes he returns to his old self. Likewise, research suggests that marital conflict erupts most frequently soon after exhausted workers arrive home, before they have had any dinner.

When I was newly pregnant with my second child, I encountered the biggest wave of anger of my life. I was mad at my husband for something he'd done. While it wasn't illegal or immoral, it was something I considered unimaginable. Looking back, I can see that part of my reaction was due to the hormonal changes going on in me. At the time, I was so mad I didn't sleep for several nights. I'd see him in the kitchen and start burning with anger. He would ask me a question, and I would fire back a catty or sarcastic remark. I was furious and didn't know what to do with it.

Finally I opened up to my acupuncturist about the situation. After I described what was going on, he said in a straightforward manner, "You are going to have to drop it." He went on to explain,

> Qi [energy] is a finite resource, and whether the work of the moment is mental, physical, or emotional, we have only so much Qi to give it. The student who applies herself to her books all day is no less fatigued than the worker digging trenches. If we let our emotions run riot, it consumes our Qi and depletes us, sapping our vitality and leaving us more prone to imbalance.[1]

That meant that if I spent three hours of my day steaming and repeating, "I am so mad, I can't believe he did that," then my body had less energy for growing the baby inside.

As I listened, I thought to myself, "That makes sense, but how the heck do I do that?" I knew my body needed the energy that was being directed into the anger, but I also knew the energy of this anger was so big it was going to be a real challenge to drop it. Desperate for a new way, I tried to implement his suggestion. Again and again over the next few weeks, whenever anger arose, I did my best to let it go. No figuring it out, no long mental debates or running through retaliation scenarios. I just dropped it. It worked. Eventually the fire of the situation fizzled, and I could move on.

---

[1] Don Gates, conversation with author, March 12, 2009.

Learning a new way to work with anger was no easy task, but it was well worth it. My baby was born healthy and strong, and I had a new tool in my toolbox for the many exhausted days when anger would arise and I could choose to put my energy into something more productive.

Growing up, what did you learn to do when anger emerged in you, or someone around you? What techniques have you tried for dealing with it? Which ones work best?

32 The Neutral Zone

William Bridges, in *Transitions: Making Sense of Life's Changes*, writes about the three phases of any life transition: the ending, the neutral zone, and new beginnings. While we may or may not have initiated or welcomed an ending, we have a choice about how we move through the neutral zone on our way to a new beginning. Our fast-paced culture often encourages us to zoom through these endings and beginnings. However, we can gain a lot by lingering in the neutral zone. Bridges writes:

> You should not feel defensive about this apparently unproductive time-out during your transition points, for the neutral zone is meant to be a moratorium from the conventional activity of your everyday existence.[1]

---

[1] William Bridges, *Transitions: Making Sense of Life's Changes*, 2nd ed. (Cambridge, MA: Da Capo Press, 2004), 135.

These words make me think about the Jewish tradition of sitting Shiva, when family members halt most of their outside activities to enter a period of mourning, a time for friends and family to gather. It also brings to mind the afternoon or evening walks that many people used to have between home and work or work and school. For me this walk gave space to shift from school friends and work to home and neighbors, with a mile-long expanse in the middle.

In my late twenties I decided to pack up my life and move from Boston to California. But right after I packed up my Boston apartment and before my 3,000-mile move, a work opportunity arose even further away—in Australia. I jumped at the chance. I remember looking out the window as we flew out over the Pacific, seeing the edge of the California coast, and saying goodbye to what I had known of my life so far. I was literally flying into the unknown, since I'd never been further west than California.

I landed at the end of the thirteen-hour journey and then spent three weeks in a kind of limbo between the old life and the new. I remember feeling a bit disoriented but also excited by the freedom in having just a few material possessions, no interactions with people I knew, and minimal obligations. After a few days of work, I had two weeks off to do whatever I wanted. During this interlude I did a lot of wandering—down roads, into stores, in books, and with my journal. Much of this wandering felt luxurious and adventure-filled, but some of it raised anxiety.

One night, in the middle of a torrential rainstorm, staying in a hut at a yoga-based retreat center, I freaked out. Realizing I had let go of my work, my apartment, and my hometown, my body began sending me strong signals of danger. My thoughts began turning to how I could get off this continent as fast as possible and move things in my life forward either by reversing all my decisions, or moving rapidly into the new life that I hoped to create in California. I spent several hours experiencing the monsters of insecurity and anxiety straight on.

The next day, after I had thoroughly researched flights home and found only dead ends, I made my way to a yoga class and released the tensions my body had been holding. I recommitted to staying in Australia until the end of my trip. Although I didn't have the language for it at the time, I was acknowledging the neutral zone, and allowing myself to stay in it.

What unfolded over the next week was something of a miracle. It's a long story and I won't tell it here, but the result was finding the man I would marry a little more than a year later. Staying in the unknown, not fleeing to my new life, I was able to see aspects of myself that I had been denying all my adult life. Even experiencing the fear while I was in that neutral zone proved a valuable experience for my future.

Are you approaching or in the middle of a transition? Can you make space for a neutral zone as something ends and something new emerges? What might support you to stay in this space of not knowing?

33 Sniggling

When I was little, I spent hundreds of hours in our basement. We lived in a 200-year-old house with a dark musty basement that was totally unfinished. We kids owned the space. My three brothers, my little sister, my friends, and I played endless hours of house or store or school. We painted and created plays and made up our own rules for floor hockey.

Today most kids and adults have very little open-ended, unstructured time. Time that my friend KP calls "sniggling." For her, sniggling evokes that single-woman Saturday morning when she could lie in bed and read until ten o'clock, then get dressed in her favorite clothes and walk to the farmer's market in Minneapolis where she bumped into a friend who wanted to grab a cup of coffee. When she introduced me to this process, I found it a new and breakthrough concept. I was a hard-driving workaholic who got up at seven on Saturday morning to take a run, shower, and dive into extra work I wanted to get done before Monday. But as I inched my way into spending time KP's way, I grew addicted. It was a great new drug!

Research on managers at work and children at play concludes that unstructured time is good for both individual people and organizations. Here are a few reasons why:

- It helps people figure out what they like and need (I can't tell you how many people I've coached who, when asked, don't know what they want).
- It's an opportunity to practice making decisions based on your own interests and ideas (not your parents' or boss's).
- It makes people happy.
- It promotes focus because no one is telling you to move on to the next thing.
- It opens a space where innovation and new ideas are born.

Julia Cameron, author of *The Artist's Way*, suggests a similar practice. She encourages what she calls "the artist date."[1] On an artist date you take your inner artist out on a date with the intention to fill up your internal well of inspiration and ideas, which in turn get poured back out through you when you are ready to create. I found that sniggling often ended up being just the artist date I needed. I didn't need the inspiration from a museum (which many artists might choose); I needed the

---

[1] Julia Cameron, *The Artist's Way: A Spiritual Path to Higher Creativity* (New York: Putnam, 1992), 18-20.

inspiration of the fabrics I found in my closet and the visual concepts I picked up at the coffee shop down the road. As an informal artist, I needed informal creative inspiration.

I designate certain days as "do-nothing days." In effect, the intention is to plan unstructured time into our schedules. And it's best not to cut it too short. It often takes an hour or two for people to settle into themselves. No video games or TV, just time to find that forgotten toy, play a board game, or bake something we think about because we looked in the pantry and seeing the cornmeal got us thinking. Once I learned how to sniggle, I found it easy to love my kids. My eight-year-old son goes off to his room for two hours and comes back with an amazing drawing of the cars he loves; my daughter creates a veterinarian shop in her room and invites us all to play a hurt animal and come for a visit. These days don't happen frequently enough, or always end in harmony, but it's always easy to see their benefit.

What is your relationship to unstructured time? How might you have a bit of it in your day today?

34 Life in Chapters

One of my favorite books is *A Woman's Book of Life: The Biology, Psychology, and Spirituality of the Feminine Life Cycle* by Joan Borysenko. This book has helped me think about living life in chapters. In it Borysenko divides the lifespan into seven-year intervals and explores the biological, psychological, and spiritual development that is common for women in each phase.

In "The Midlife Metamorphosis," which covers ages forty-two to forty-nine, Borysenko describes the birth of the inner Guardian:

> Those of us, who have accomplished enough of our personal healing to reach emotional maturity by the end of the first half of life, enter the second half with a remarkable burst of new energy.[1]

---

[1] Joan Borysenko, *A Woman's Book of Life: The Biology, Psychology, and Spirituality of the Feminine Life Cycle* (New York: Riverhead Books, 1996), 153.

Reading this as a much younger woman gave me a sigh of relief, "Oh, I don't have to do all this healing in my twenties; there may be much more time for it all to happen." Reading it again in my forties, I felt a sense of recognition, a sense that, "Yeah, I can feel some new energy emerging after fifteen years of searching, experiencing, and healing."

Whether you are male or female, it can be helpful to think about life in this stage-by-stage way. First, it means we don't have to do it all right now. If we frame what we are doing as something that works in this chapter of life, it's easier to be hopeful about doing something different in the next chapter. It's easier to be at peace with what is happening now because it doesn't have to be like this forever.

In *The 7 Stages of Motherhood: Loving Your Life without Losing Your Mind*, author Ann Pleshette Murphy asks, "How do you attend to your own developmental needs at each stage of your child's life? And why is that so important?"[2] Even if you are not a parent, you can reframe this question to fit any identity that is important to you. How do you attend to your own developmental needs at each stage of your career? Or each stage of your creative life? Murphy's question highlights that we are in continuous motion and that things both inside us and external to us keep changing.

---

[2] Ann Pleshette Murphy, *The 7 Stages of Motherhood: Making the Most of Your Life as a Mom* (New York: Alfred A. Knopf, 2004), xi.

Considering our lives and our development one stage at a time offers space to examine the details more closely and remind us that life is not about arriving somewhere, but the journey along the way.

How would you name the chapter you are in now? Can you feel yourself in the beginning, middle, or end? How might thinking of yourself in relationship to this chapter help you make sense of what you do today or this week?

35 Doing Something Really Well

I keep a mental list of my encounters with excellence. Brunch at the Ritz Carlton in Half Moon Bay is on it, along with the work experience I had when I worked in partnership with a team at Bain & Company in Boston years ago. Also on the list are my first Mac computer and the children's TV series "Peep and the Big Wide World."

I remember a cup of vanilla ice cream I had at the Bent Spoon, a tiny ice cream shop in Princeton, New Jersey. With each mouthful, I could almost taste the attention to detail and the carefully chosen local ingredients. The tiny wooden spoon reminded me to savor the small portion. The roster of flavors, handwritten on a chalkboard above the long line of waiting customers, inspired whimsy and creativity.

When I try to imagine achieving that level of excellence myself or paying that kind attention to detail, I despair. In most areas of my life, it feels far out of reach.

One day I asked my friend Mary how she pulled off Christmas dinner with such perfection and grace every year. "I stick to the same thing and do it over and over," she replied. That was a foreign idea. After that I started watching other women I admire. They too seem to pick something (a routine, a recipe, a job) and do it repeatedly, gaining more confidence and capacity along the way.

Unfortunately, this strategy of repetition hasn't worked for me yet. My creative personality wants to change everything all the time. I rearrange the house every season. If I make a monthly meal schedule for my family, I'm ready for a new one before the end of the first month. Still, I think people who follow and perfect a routine are onto something, something that I'd like to learn.

Lately I've discovered that it helps to partner with the right people. My newest work partner has high standards for her work. She is methodical. She encourages those who work with her to put double or triple time into planning a meeting or event. Afterward, her follow-up captures all of the details of a meeting we've facilitated, which she presents graphically in a professional and thoughtful way. Working with her always slows me down. While I can fly by the seat of my pants and get away with it, I don't always enjoy just squeaking by. When I'm in the middle of a project, I can see that had I put in more prep time, the project might have turned out better.

In addition to slowing down, another result of this partnership is that I'm having a blast. I feel good about our consulting and facilitation work. I'm starting to put more preparation time into my home life as well. I'm noticing that if I line up more activities for the kids on the weekend, instead of just waking up Saturday morning and figuring out a plan, things go better. I'm learning to be more realistic about what it takes to implement an idea or project.

I'm also finding that doing something really well can be addictive. Once you start doing it, you want more. It reminds me of the way I felt when I left the Bent Spoon. I was completely satisfied by the amazing cup of burnt caramel ice cream and already looking forward to the next one.

What do you do really well? Is there something else you want to do really well? What do you need to move toward a higher level of excellence in some area?

36 Find the Right Incentives

Tom Rath and Jim Harter, researchers at the Gallup Institute, studied massive amounts of global research to try to understand wellbeing—what constitutes it, how wellbeing in one area of our lives affects other areas, and what we can do to improve it. In looking at the habits of tens of thousands of people, they concluded, "If we can find *short-term incentives that are consistent with our long-term objectives*, it is much easier to make the right decisions in the moment."[1]

Kind of a simple, common-sense idea, but one that's not so easy to put into action.

When I was trying to finish this book I found it difficult to keep up the pace that I had set for myself. Though I really wanted to meet my deadline, I kept hitting a wall with my energy. With just a week left and lots of work

---

[1] Tom Rath and Jim Harter, *Wellbeing: The Five Essential Elements* (New York: Gallup Press, 2010), 9.

to do, my writer friend Diane suggested, "Give yourself a reward every time you write." So, just like I do for the kids, I made a sticker chart and hung it in the kitchen for all to see. For every hour worked on the book, I'd get a sticker. Then, when the chart was complete, I would get to buy a stylish new workout shirt. At the end of the week, I had done it. Looking back I knew that some days I was writing for the satisfaction of the work; on other days it was all about the shirt.

I find this approach also works well for my fitness goals. I want to be strong, healthy, and in top physical condition. To achieve this, rather than focusing on the long journey from my out-of-shape body to the buff one I envision, I focus on working out every day. Sometimes I walk with a friend; sometimes I practice yoga. Sometimes I just move. Daily exercise always improves my mood and energy, and the momentum I feel after just a few days of working out actually becomes my incentive. Rather than feeling stuck because I missed running a few miles, I'm thrilled because I danced around my living room with my kids until my heart was pumping hard.

Applying this strategy to writing deadlines and exercise goals is familiar to many people. But what if we also use it for our emotional, financial, or social goals? This week my son gets one minute of video time for every minute he meditates, and I get a cookie for every hour I spend writing. We'll see how it goes.

Pick an area of wellbeing that you would like to improve. (Rath and Harter suggest: Career, Physical, Social, Financial, or Community.) If you are clear about the long-term goal in your chosen area, what might be a short-term incentive that rewards you for the actions required to get you there?

37 Get off the Sidelines

One fall morning, I sat watching a line of six-year-olds on a soccer field. They stood single file in front of a pee-wee-sized goal, taking shots on the adult goalie. One by one they dribbled forward, took a shot, and missed. Kid after kid kicked a ball that went flying off to the side of the field. Every once in a while, a shot made it into the goal. Regardless of the outcome, though, the kids happily bounded back to the end of the line, waiting for their next chance to try. Their success rate didn't seem to affect their enthusiasm or effort. They were there to play.

Sitting on the sidelines I wondered, "When do most of us lose this quality of being able to just go for it?"

For my birthday one year my friend Claudia gave me a copy of *My Year with Eleanor*, by Noelle Hancock. At almost thirty, the author suddenly lost her on-line blogging job. Inspired by Roosevelt's example, she then decided to embark on a yearlong journey to take on one thing each day that scared her.

While I am not chomping at the bit to swim with sharks (which the author did) or fly a plane in simulated combat (which she also did), there are dozens of things I want to do but am afraid to try. I want to start a popcorn shop, host a formal Renaissance Ball, and write an article for a prominent magazine. Too often I stop myself from acting on these desires because I don't want to fail.

Support from others helps me overcome this fear of failing. When three good friends agreed to train with me for the New York Marathon, I finally took it on (after years of thinking about it). Finding a new business partner gave me the courage to move out of nonprofit and philanthropic consulting and into the corporate world.

Framing a challenge in a new way can also help. Taking my cue from the six-year-olds on the soccer field, I learned the value of letting go of the score and started paying attention to each shot. When faced with raising $100,000 in one month for the nonprofit I ran, I shifted my attention from finding donors to getting as many people as I could to say no to my request for funding. If I was getting the nos, it meant I was in the game and playing hard. That allowed me to pick up the phone day after day, rather than be immobilized by repeated disappointment. I was taking the shot. Even when I missed the goal, I was participating, no longer sitting on the sidelines.

Is there some area of your life in which you are sitting on the sidelines, wanting to get more fully in the game? How does it feel? What might it take to make a step toward greater engagement?

38 **What's the Story?**

I like to begin each January with an intention for the year. A few years ago I resolved to be less constrained and allow my passions greater expression. I had observed how disciplined I had become with food, exercise, and social time and could see that in my effort to not overextend myself, my world had become boring.

As I started acting on this intention, I noticed that my desire for sugar and caffeine dramatically increased. Because of my intention, I allowed myself to indulge in both, which ignited a deep craving for more. I hadn't known how much I missed them. One day I grabbed a chocolate-covered, creme-filled Hostess Yodel, pausing and breathing into the strong desire I had to eat it. As I tore open the white plastic and a thin layer of chocolate coating fell out of the bag, I realized I wasn't just immersed in the flavor and texture of the little cake in front of me, I was breathing in the history it represented.

When I was ten, our walk home from school passed by Sunden's Farm, a corner farm stand and convenience store. I can still picture myself walking down the farm's sloped driveway with my three brothers, eagerly anticipating the day's treat. I felt a familiar anxiety about the choice I would make. Would it be an old-fashioned candy stick, a Hostess Snowball, an ice cream sandwich? As I let myself imagine the old scene my body warmed at the feeling of connection. That after-school time holds some of my most cherished childhood memories: racing to the stoplight, walking and talking about silly things, forming a big gang with the other neighborhood kids who walked home with us.

Critical feelings about myself for eating junk food quickly transformed into a sweet communion with my past and a deep desire to be with my brothers more often in the coming year. As a result, I decided to write them an email suggesting that we get together.

Who would have guessed that story would be hidden inside the Yodel wrapper.

At a different time in my life I hosted what we called Soul Food Potlucks. Each had a theme, and people brought food to fit the theme. Themes ranged from "Gourmet Versions of Your Childhood Favorite" to "Foods within the Rainbow" and "Foods that Relate to the Letter C." During the potluck we raised a question for conversation, and those who were inspired to respond did. Questions included: What is feeding you right now? Or, how are the personal and political tied together in your life? Often, we noticed profound connections between the foods that people brought and the stories they told.

At an annual retreat of one of my client organizations, facilitators encouraged participants to bring an object for the opening gathering. Each item was passed around a circle of ten people, who each could connect to the object and make a guess about why that person might have chosen it. People brought photos, sticks, religious symbols, and other objects. After making the circle the object landed in front of its owner, who then told a story about the object and it's significance in their life. That simple process led to profound relationship building; many participants identified it as the favorite part of the retreat.

There are stories connected to so many of the things we eat, activities we do, and objects we own. Slowing down to hear them can be worth the time.

Look around the space you are in right now. Do you see something that has a story connected to it? What is the story?

39 Managing Energy

Centered Leadership: How Talented Women Thrive, a report by three women who worked with the consulting firm McKinsey & Company, outlines five competencies necessary for successful women to thrive. I was taken aback to see that they listed "managing energy" as one of the five.

Two things struck me immediately. First, I hadn't seen the concept of energy management discussed in a mainstream, business-oriented publication before. Second, I can't think of a competency more relevant for people who are trying to keep up with a fast-paced work environment and simultaneously keep things together at home.

My strong reaction to the report got me musing:

- How much attention do I give to managing my energy?

- Do I know what is depleting my energy these days?
- What gives me energy?
- How do I use my energy when I'm fueled up?

With these questions in mind, I headed to a meeting one day. I was full of energy, excited about the project we were going to discuss, and ready for the work it would take to implement it. But after the meeting, I felt deflated, flat as a tire. My excitement for the project had escaped along with my energy. The questions about energy management were still swirling in my head. They got me curious. I wondered why I had gone from high energy to zero in less than an hour.

As I reflected on the details of the meeting, I noticed that the person I met with had been full of anxiety about the event we were planning. It was obvious in her words and her body language. During the meeting her anxiety spilled over onto me, and I, too, began to worry about how the event would go, whether people would show up, and how it would reflect on me if it didn't go well.

With this insight, I wrote an email to my colleague addressing the anxiety and asking if we could rethink our approach so it might be less stressful for her. I also reassessed my role, my expectations for the event, and my own related anxiety. With this action I was able to interrupt the cycle of anxiety. I remembered that this was a low priority event for me. I also reminded myself I had little control over the event and recognized that I was fully on top of my responsibilities connected to it. As a result, my energy bounced back and so did my excitement for the project.

A person's "energy" is often a major determining factor in their success in professional as well as personal situations. Regardless of what you are doing, how are you being? Is your energy grounded in a way that helps people around you relax? Do you have energy to do all that you have taken on, or do you show up depleted on a regular basis? When your energy is high, do you focus it well on the things that matter the most? There are so many questions we could ask ourselves that relate to this topic. Although it's an invisible dimension of leadership, it's a critical one. One that belongs in the limelight.

How would you describe your energy in this moment? In general, how aware are you of your energy and how it's affecting you or others around you? Is there something you could do today or this week to become more aware of your energetic state and how you respond to it?

40 Flexibility

Sometimes when people hear that I am a yoga teacher, they respond with a comment like "I could never do yoga. I'm the most inflexible person in the world." I assure them that I am, too. I've never been one of those yogis who can twist into a pretzel position or even touch my toes. Being uncomfortable in my body was my natural pre-yoga state. I worked for years before I felt any ease with my practice. Having lots of self-compassion was the only way through. I had to love myself and my body even when it felt tight and resistant. As a result of this experience, I often think of myself as a yoga teacher for non-yogis.

Yoga comes to mind when I think about practicing flexibility in life. In both yoga and life some people are more able to shift plans, adjust their expectations, and move along easily. Others find change more challenging, requiring great effort and practice.

Off the yoga mat, shifting plans and making adjustments is relatively easy for me. Sometimes too easy. Some of my former colleagues complained that they never knew what to expect from me. If we mapped out a strategic plan one day, I might get additional input the next day and completely revise the plan. This drove some of those colleagues crazy. In other contexts my flexibility was welcomed. This was the case when the people I was working with appreciated that I could generate a wealth of creative solutions to a problem without being attached to any single idea.

In my thirties, I learned the value of flexibility in relation to my health. My pattern was to keep going even when I got sick with bronchitis or a chest cold. I was so used to powering through that I hardly missed a day of work. But one winter, this approach led to weeks of sickness and a cough that lasted for several months. An ah-ha moment happened one day that winter when I was so sick I had to stay in bed. I was exhausted but had a tight deadline, so I kept trying to sit up and complete the task I had promised to deliver. A friend who called to check on me was so alarmed by my behavior that she insisted, "You are sick! Change the deadline and it will be fine."

Such a basic, obvious statement would sound rational to most people. But to me, it was a revelation. For years afterward I struggled to accept illness as a reason to readjust my expectations for what I could accomplish. I struggled to communicate my changing needs to others and to not worry too much about their reactions, positive or negative. Over time I found incredible freedom from accepting the limits imposed by illness.

Learning how to be flexible has also served me well as a parent and a partner. The thousands of unanticipated events I've had to manage as a parent constantly call upon my ability to readjust and communicate. But I'm not always flexible. After I relocated to California it took me years to realize how much I missed people and how often I need to travel back East for visits. An outsider might have said I wasted years grieving and being stuck, but I now understand that adjustment takes time. It took me years to let it go and move on. I was just like that tight hamstring that won't let go.

For others, who are more methodical and less flexible by nature, facing change can be disorienting, infuriating, and disappointing. For them, even more self-compassion is needed. Just like in yoga, if your body happens to be one that is not like a rubber band, you may need more practice and more understanding as you struggle through the motions.

When do you find it easy to shift plans and make adjustments? When is this process difficult?

41 The Adaptive Path

I remember the day I made a conscious decision to get off the Fast Track. I had just gotten into Harvard's Graduate School of Education. The night before I had spent another of many nights crying myself to sleep over my partner-less, childless status. I knew that if I really wanted to find a partner and be a mother, my life needed some major shaking up. Jumping back into the high achievement-oriented world of Harvard was not the way forward. The work-dominated life I had been living, while rewarding up until then, was not going to get me what I wanted most. With a phone number for a vacant room in Berkeley, California, in hand, I was ready for something new.

What I didn't know at the time was that this departure from the Fast Track would lead to such a different landscape. Two years after I made that decision I sat holding a newborn, with my husband of a year, in our home in the suburbs outside San Francisco. I had downshifted from a position as the Director of Training to something that felt just a tad bit higher than a telemarketer. Instead of studying at Harvard, I had enrolled in a small Catholic college I had never heard of to do a graduate program in leadership. I had not only left the freeway, I had jumped the side barrier and headed into a vast landscape. Unknown territory was my new reality.

Being adaptive and reflecting on what was happening in my work and my home became the new way forward. While moving through this territory required a new level of creativity and patience, it proved to be empowering and rewarding.

I did not get on the mommy track and opt out of work. I loved my work. Even though I was passionate about parenting, I needed work for creative expression, relationships, social impact, and to satiate my intellectual curiosity. I did my best to keep my work life going at a pace that felt manageable. As an independent consultant, I was able to arrange to work twenty hours a week, most of the time.

Unfortunately, our organizational world is not very well set up to support this path. There are many people who would prefer a rewarding part-time job, but their organizations either don't offer or don't allow it. This wastes talents in two ways. Some people, faced with this lack of choice, opt out. Others stay in. They power through, but end up feeling unsatisfied and exhausted.

In some professions, alternatives to the forty-hour workweek are well established. Some nurses and veterinarians have a three-day-a-week schedule. Consultants and writers can often increase or decrease their hours as needed. But for the vast majority, these options still aren't available.

As for my path, I'm currently accelerating and attempting to merge back onto the highway. It's not always easy. Sometimes I have to create my own on-ramps. I'm not going anywhere near the fast lane, but I feel confident enough to reenter the flow of traffic and travel at my own speed, even if it means being pulled over and given a ticket for going too slow.

What choices have you made or do you imagine making about your work life? Is there a version of a fast track, an opting out, or an adaptive path in your work or life context? How do you feel about where you are?

42 A Wholehearted Life

Last summer, I got to spend some time with my oldest brother, John. We had a rare hour to kayak across the salt pond where we'd spent our summers growing up. During our journey we appreciated the warm sun and the gulls flying above. As I paddled, memories from our childhood came to mind—water skiing at dawn, swimming with my clan of buddies, jumping off Rock Island, and fishing for flounder.

Halfway through the trip the conversation turned to my dad, whom we both admired immensely. He had been very sick, and we were both worried that it might be our last year with him.

John talked about how my dad's example pushed him to be his best as a father. Toward the end of the conversation he said, "You know, Dad always said to put it all on the table. Give it everything you've got. Then when it's time for you to go, you will know you've done the best you could." John went on to say, "I think Dad's at peace because he knows he has done that. I guess that's what I'm trying to do too."

At a recent party, I spoke to a woman who clearly lives this way. Rosa is an artist. When I asked about her life, she told me, "Life is great. We have no money, but we've never had money, so we are used to it. I'm working on a novel, and it's exciting and juicy and life is good." She went on to talk about how grateful she was for her partner and her daughter. She moved from guest to guest at the party, greeting them and laughing. She hugged hard and smiled broadly as she reached for my daughter's painted fingernails. Rosa held up the newly knitted scarf around her own neck and celebrated her first attempt at knitting. She, too, was full in, walking a wholehearted path.

In line at Safeway a couple of days later, I wondered what I would find if I looked for the ways each one of us is attempting that wholeheartedness in our lives. I noticed how much the cashier really cared about people donating to the store's Toys for Tots campaign and how sweetly the bagger was talking with my daughter as he loaded the groceries in the bag. It was a good reminder that even when we can't manage a whole life that feels wholehearted, we can pick one thing and really go for it.

One time when I was feeling particularly exhausted, I was inspired to plan and host a party with my son, who was turning seven. I noticed that even though I was really tired, when the time came to work on the party,

I lit up and dove in. I gave the project my all. Together we searched the Internet for spy games. I recruited other parents to put on disguises during the party, and I raced to the party store looking for spy kit materials. While much of me felt less than wholehearted, this one spot in me felt fully alive and engaged, and that felt great.

In what area of your life are you living in a wholehearted way? How does it feel?

Acknowledgements

This book is the product of ten years of musing about life, so there are many people to thank whose contributions collectively made this work possible. Liane Louie-Badua, Haru Inouye, Nan Peterson, and the staff and network of the Shinnyo-en Foundation deepened my understanding of and commitment to reflective practice. Dean Elias, Ken Otter, Doug Paxton, Ann Marie Foley, Tammy Appling-Cabading, and Paul Loper of the Saint Mary's College of California's Leadership Studies Program introduced me to the practice of the reflective paper and, in doing so, inspired the form of this book. Each has been a critical supporter as I developed my thinking and practice.

My uncle, Borden Mace, told me I had something good when I showed him a very early draft of this book. His encouragement, which has been around since he taught me to count to 100, was a critical part of my decision to share my writing in public. The women who have helped to take care of my children during this journey have been invaluable, both by making my writing time possible and by serving as much-needed sounding boards. They include Christina Ivonowski, Katie Irwin, Rebecca Stevenson, Eliot Jackson, Sandra Ramirez, Meghan Whitbred, and Leah Hendricks-Smith. Many friends have listened, edited, and encouraged: Kitty Benedict, Kathleen Brown, Katrina Browne, Susan Bacher, AJ Brown, Kelly Corrigan, April Cotte, Diane Hackett, Cathy Harris, Mona Johnson, Mel King, Ann Kletz, Johnnie Lewis, Celia Marinier, Madeline McNeeley, Sarah Mermin, Sara Mooradian, Monica Moore, Betsy Myers, Jenny Sazama, Katie Pakos Rimer and Ned Rimer, Dustie Robeson, Edy and Jeff Schwartz, Ashley Sloat, Julie Stiles, Megan Voorhees, Bette Walker, and Jesse White. All who have attended the Mindful Moms group have inspired me to keep writing. And so many others who support me in a million visible and invisible ways.

When I received Julia Scatliff O'Grady's book, *Good Busy*, in the mail, I felt the possibility of writing a book like it. Her gracious encouragement to approach her publisher, Jeanette Stokes at RCWMS Press, led to a rich partnership. Deep thanks to Julia and to the women who worked with my words. Jeanette Stokes and Marcy Litle are masterful editors; I can't thank them enough. Kaudie McLean, Jocelyn Streid, and Liz Dowling-Sendor did meticulous proofreading. For the cover art and graphic design, I am grateful for Pati Reis of Designing Solutions.

My family, who have helped to create the life that I write about, have been my grounding place. Thank you to Noel, my fabulous, loving husband. And to Will and Ellie, the beautiful children who are growing me up. Mom, Dad, John, Wenley, Rich, Kelly, Brendan, Laura, Katie, Kevin, Nancy, Billy, Sarah, Arrington, Hez, Nevaeh, and all my extended family, thanks for being the bedrock of what matters most to me.

Claudia Horwitz has been talking with me once a week over the course of this book's life. She has helped me clarify my visions, held me accountable to self-imposed deadlines, and asked the needed and critical questions. I'm so grateful for all that she has offered.